D0576968

"Long after the sites profiled here are little more than errant electron clouds in th

# Graphis Web Design Now 1

An International Survey of Web Design

Edited by Ken Coupland
Art Directed and Designed by Robert Appleton

ther, the trajectory of innovation they reveal in this book will remain." Paul Saffo

Publisher and Creative Director, B. Martin Pedersen

2000 2001 2002

Writer, Ken Coupland
Art Director and Designer, Robert Appleton
Editorial Assistant, Margaret Smith
Design Assistants, Joseph Hom, Jonathan Lee,
Peggy Chuang and Sophie Chin
Interactive and Web Design Assistant, Betsy Chung
Data Manager, Milton Melendez

Graphis U.S., Inc. New York, Graphis Press Corp. Zurich (Switzerland)

100 communion

took on new dimensions Se
a documented constant throug
llowing the civil rights move
in progressive urban centers,
anctioned, honored and even
discovering its individual hum
with a price, as it always has.

SMART

| | Editor's Note | by Ken Coupland | 11_ |
|---|---|---|---|
| **Part One** | **The Weird Wild WWW** | Virtual communities \| innovation | 13_ |
| **Part Two** | **Designers** | Self promotion \| portfolios | 17_ |
| **Part Three** | **Repurposing Media** | Digizines \| other media | 83_ |
| **Part Four** | **The Corporate Sector** | Sales \| marketing \| promotion | 127_ |
| **Part Five** | **Arts and Experimental** | Perspective \| vocabulary | 161_ |
| | Interviews | Thirteen Designers | 193 |

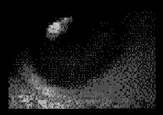

Welcome to the World Wide Web, the fastest-growing medium – or rather, near-medium – on the planet today. For the Web remains a raw, untamed technology that is struggling to become a mature means of communication. This transformation-in-the-making has been responsible for its share of what can only be called cybercrud. But buried in all the crud there are a growing number of media gems – elegant and compelling Web destinations that foreshadow the aesthetic trajectory of this emerging medium. The very best of these destinations, and the designers who created them, are detailed in the pages that follow. This book is more, however, than merely a beauty contest for a medium in the making. It is a practicum of ideas from those on the vanguard of change. Here you can not only see the results, you can also read about the logic and vision behind the design. Meanwhile, the Web continues to evolve and grow at warp speed. By the time these words are printed, many of these sites will have changed beyond recognition, and some may have disappeared. This has the smell of anathema to the web-smitten. After all, why examine the ghosts of old pages when there are new novelties waiting to be explored in cyberspace? My answer to that is, as it turns out, that knowing where you come from goes a long way to helping you figure out where you are headed. The contents of this book offer a snapshot of the very best design the Web has to offer at a critical moment in time. True design excellence reveals itself eventually, as the stuff of fads erodes away. As you read these pages, reflect on what was momentary fancy, and what has become bedrock for a new media edifice. Then visit the website for the book to see what the 'latest' has evolved into. One of the most interesting aspects of the Web is how old and new intersect in surprising and delightful ways. This is the essence of design in a digital age, to apply the best of old media sensibilities to the service of creating novel and compelling new media experiences. Of course, too often we do the reverse, blindly applying bad old media habits to create intellectual 'horseless carriages' in the new medium. It is an unavoidable part of the media creation process: Early radio copied theater, TV tried to simulate movies, and once upon a time Web designers were happy to treat their medium as a mere simulacrum of paper. This is already changing, as the Web continues to reinvent itself on its way to becoming a medium. Over the next couple of years, three changes will change the Web profoundly, and as usual, designers will be at Ground Zero. First, we will shift from two-dimensional 'pages' to three-dimensional 'spaces.' Second, information on the Web will cease to be inert. An increasing proportion will become active: animated, immediate, and in the long-run, autonomous. And finally, the Web as an information medium will yield to the Web as an interpersonal medium. Where once we sought information, we will now engage in conversation with other humans and eventually, with computer intelligences as well, with information playing a supporting role. The Web is a shape-shifter, and that is what makes it so fascinating. 'Surfing' the Web seemed so hip just a year or two ago, but a year or two from now, it will seem as ancient a concept as dancing the Charleston or doing the twist. Instead, we will fly through information spaces and look forward to teleporting into social virtual realities. And a few years further down the road, those novelties will fall before yet newer metaphors. But through it all, one constant will remain: the values of excellent design in the service of sense-making and human connection. Long after the sites profiled here are little more than errant electron clouds in the ether, the trajectory of innovation they reveal in this book will remain.

Paul Saffo is a director of the Menlo Park, California-based Institute of the Future, where he spends

his time trying to make sense of emerging technologies.

As a publisher, it has been my great pleasure to produce many books that I am proud of. They are all labors of love, and since I am a designer by profession, I am acutely aware of the contributions of editors and designers and the creative synergy that is necessary to make a book a success. That synergy has never been greater, or the task more daunting, than with Web Design Now. The Web is exploding. Which sites are 'state of the art?' Are they pretty, Are they functional? Are they interactive and importantly, are they successful? Do they accomplish their tasks in a way that contributes to a company's image and goals? I couldn't have had two better professionals to answer these questions. Ken Coupland is the Editor of Web Design Now. An accomplished journalist with a background in new technology, Ken was the leader in determining which sites should be considered for inclusion. He shaped the book and provided a context for images and sites to be evaluated. He provided the extraordinary perspective that was necessary to keep the book focused and balanced. Robert Appleton is the Designer and Art Director whose talent has made this book come to life. Much more than a stylist, his original vision has brought clarity and insight. He visited each of the sites Ken provided, suggesting new ones, delving into their content, choosing the most stimulating material – then editing, pacing and structuring that into a book which he filled with interactive surprise (his flick book alone, encouraged us to create this new Graphis soft-cover). It was also Bob's suggestion to include Part Five, Arts and Experimental, for which he has written an introduction. As you review Web Design Now, we hope that you enjoy the fruits of their labor (and ours), and that you are inspired to create even better web sites. And when you do, we'll be looking for you. Regards, B. Martin Pedersen, Publisher

Mention to anyone with the slightest interest in the subject that you're editing a book on design for the World Wide Web

and you're likely to be met with bewilderment, or maybe even derision. Why a book, after all, about a medium

that is supposed to be replacing the printed page? Besides, isn't the Web – as Paul Saffo noted earlier – undergoing

a frenetic rate of change? Surely any book on the topic, by the time it is published, will be hopelessly out of date.

Well, first, as the volume you hold in your hands should prove, books aren't about to disappear any time soon. In fact,

as many have pointed out, books are being published in greater numbers than ever before. Only the most

starry-eyed new media zealots expect the Web to replace print; most merely expect it will augment print, leaving books

to do what they do best. In this case, that means providing a handy comprehensive visual 'map' of many diverse

design possibilities. Secondly, the Web is changing, and rapidly. Although this book was written, edited, designed and

printed with what is – by traditional publishing standards – blinding speed, what you see here can only

represent the Web at a certain point in time, specifically, the Spring of 1997. How good a picture, then, does it provide?

To begin with, let me note that, in several ways, this book was created and produced a little differently from

most Graphis titles. Most importantly, instead of announcing a call for entries and waiting for submissions, we tracked

down and checked out every website we could find that we thought might have some visual merit. We followed

up numerous tips, plundered awards sites and ran down links from studios of interest. We also had a very gratifying

response from the design community to our questionnaires; only a handful of webmasters we contacted –

you know who you are – neglected to make a reply. (Since a reply was necessary for inclusion, you won't see their

websites here.) It should be noted, too, that the book's editorial production itself was streamlined to take

advantage of the Web. We did all the information gathering with e-mail and generated the vast majority of the images

from screen grabs taken directly off the Internet. While there were exceptions – sometimes phone calls were

the only way to clarify a point (email, in case you haven't noticed, can end up awfully discursive) and sometimes we

needed original image files for display purposes – this book was, by and large, produced entirely by electronic

means. Except for the final film, paper and ink of course. Another thing that's unusual about this book is the amount of

text we decided to include. We felt that the issues of Web design needed to be communicated by the designers

themselves, so we asked for their in-depth analysis of why and how their sites work, and we gave them plenty of room

in the back of the book to do just that. We also interviewed a dozen leading designers in the field to get a more personal perspective, and you'll find their interviews there as well. We feel this two-pronged approach – casting a wide

'net,' then zeroing in on the best people we could find – resulted in a more balanced, comprehensive and dare

we say democratic profile of Web design today than you'll see in other publications on the subject. What about the selection

process then? Well, first, we've been briefed, researching graphic design on the Web for a couple of years.

The Web is so multifarious you might think we'd have to make some agonizing decisions, ruthlessly excluding deserving

websites for space considerations and the like. Trust us, this was not the case. For proof, we asked everyone we

approached for their own suggestions. All too soon, the same Web addresses started turning up with depressing regularity.

It wasn't easy to come up with 100-odd well-designed sites. So what were our criteria? Well, visual wit and a

pleasing experience were a plus factor. Cookie-cutter solutions that simply copied tried-and-true formulas didn't excite

us. Murky deconstruction needed to be awfully appealing to make the cut. Yet at the same time we zeroed in on

dynamic websites that hinted at new directions for this rapidly developing technology. As a result, this book could be

published a year from now and it's hard to imagine how, if it all, it would look much different. Besides, many of

the websites included here are already a couple of years old - and nothing better has come along to replace them.

On the other hand, what you see here is only the tip of the iceberg. Frozen in static images, a book can only

begin to suggest what's happening with the kinetic innovations on the Web, experiments in animation and the broader

'push' technologies. And yet there's a further paradox. Right now Web technology has graphic designers in a

stranglehold. With its painfully low resolution, primitive text-handling abilities and greedy demands on visual real estate,

the medium imposes strict limitations on aesthetics. Maddeningly, the Web's potential is exploding so rapidly that,

while designers can't keep up with the new tools, the new tools themselves can't keep up with the seismic changes the

Internet is undergoing. So while this book doesn't necessarily represent what's really vital and changing about

the Web, it does show some pioneering attempts by dedicated designers to grapple with the parameters, however strict,

to engage the issues, however daunting, and to embrace a vision of what the Web will become. But now it's time

for you to go on the Web yourself, perhaps with this book in front of you as a guide. Visit the website we've created at

http://www.graphis.com with links to all the sites we've listed, and see for yourself what we're talking about.

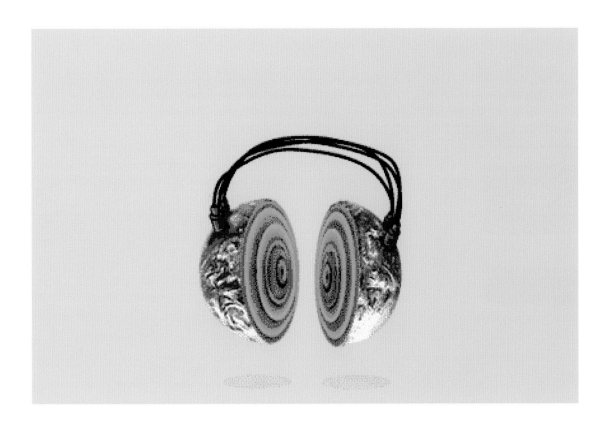

<u>The Virtual Pet</u> Home Page advertises links to websites for "virtual pets, virtual dogs, virtual cats, virtual fish, virtual birds, virtual fish tanks or a virtual aquarium." There are links for the curiously unnerving tamagochi, palm-sized, digital companions with a wretchedly short lifespan that their owners must continually play with, feed and clean up after. There are also links to find out more about 'norns', troll-like creatures whose 'brain chemistry' ebbs and flows with changing mood and circumstance, and to Phin-Phin, a slightly neurotic flying dolphin that will go away and hide for days if you speak to it harshly. From here as well, you can find out more about Kyoko Date, the nubile virtual pop star who's become something of a recording phenomenon in Japan.

<u>Strange new</u> lifeforms are taking shape on the World Wide Web, where just about anything goes as long as it's digital. Websites that allow you to create your own monstrous, customized avatars huddle cheek-and-jowl with home pages for white supremacists, for afficionados of highly specialized sexual proclivities, for apocalyptic cults. Of course, the same Web is also gearing up to be the marketplace of the twenty-first century. Smut, sports scores, and stock quotations jostle for attention with marketing pitches from every major manufacturer, media outlet and service provider. <u>**You can**</u> view the Web today through either end of the telescope. Looked at from one end, the numbers are relatively insignificant. Advertising figures – some $300 million in revenues last year - are a drop in the bucket compared with, say, the $30 billion spent on TV spots; looked at from the other, Web advertising is expected to top $5 billion (or is it $10 billion?) by the year 2000. Looked at from one end, the Web audience makes up only a tiny fraction of the mass market; looked at from the other, it's a goldmine of demographics peopled by avid consumers with unlimited purchasing power. <u>**And still**</u> the Web continues to grow. More than a million websites of all kinds have been registered to date (according to some calculations, the vast majority of them in the state of California) and thousands more are added every month. Predictions are that within a couple of years fully half of U.S. firms will have their own intranets, the term for those largely invisible in-house websites where companies conduct their day-to-day affairs. With little experience to guide them, forward-looking businesses are already grappling with the Web's awesome potential to fundamentally transform the way that companies do business.

<u>**As just**</u> about everyone in graphic design is no doubt fully aware by now, there are huge numbers of websites that need to be designed. The Web presents lucrative opportunities for those designers with the skills and talent to sidestep its limitations and capitalize on its undeniable strengths. <u>**When the**</u> Web first appeared back in the early 1990's, designers can be forgiven for experiencing a sense of déjà vu. It seemed like they'd suddenly been thrown back on the bad old days of early desktop publishing, with all its graphic - and, not least of all, typographic - crudities. At a stroke, away went the advances in type management that had accrued as desktop publishing evolved, and designers found themselves stuck with a handle of crude fonts and layouts over

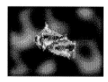

which they had no ultimate control. The situation isn't likely to change anytime soon: proper type management and format standards are still a long ways off. Worse, Web software developers have given the Macintosh platform a chilly reception, delaying upgrades in deference to PC-based versions — although designers still prefer to work on Macs. **The 'learning curve'** for Web design was not exactly 'steep' at first — rudimentary HTML is relatively easy to master — but that curve has been steadily climbing. Nowadays, Web designers — at least, those who want to keep their jobs — need to know a lot more than they may care to learn about issues like varied browser capabilities, upgrade restrictions and platform incompatibilities. Bandwidth issues plague those designers who aspire to pump large volumes of data through their sites — and will continue to plague them for some time to come. Audiences with slow modems and without the appropriate plug-ins may represent the dreaded 'lowest common denominator,' but it's one that market-savvy Web developers feel they ignore at their peril. **To further** complicate the picture, Web audiences are a fickle and contrary lot, pointedly ignoring advertising, seldom spending much time in the right places; moreover, they re proving stubbornly resistant to being led where they don't want to go. (Although the industry is understandably reluctant to admit it, visitors to some of the best-travelled websites seldom linger; half of them never make it past the front door.) Moreover, it's proving damnably difficult to figure out how to tell people where to go once they do get inside. The Web demands new guidelines, new standards for navigation and interaction, and those rules are still largely unwritten. **With all** these uncertainties, it should come as no surprise that many leading design studios, and even many advertising agencies, refuse to get involved with Web design. Yet for more adventurous graphic designers, especially those who came of age with the advent of the electronic era, the Web's possibilities seem boundless.  Already many designers are learning to use the Web to market their businesses — often, they're finding, to a far more receptive audience overseas — and even to do business over them, making presentations to clients on private, proprietary pages with shared urls. Writers, photographers and illustrators are using the Web as well, affording a low-res but seductively back-lit view of their work. **Largely unnoticed** amidst the drumbeat of excitement about the Web are the true experimenters, fearless souls who embrace its contradictions and love to play with all its latest technical gizmos. These brave pioneers are scattered around the globe, con-structing, deconstructing and reconstructing new visual metaphors for the Web. The art world, too, is starting to take notice; perceptive art dealers and museum curators are beginning to collect websites - if anything as transitory as an electronic signal over the Internet can said to be collectible. On the other hand, why not? **Yet with** all these innovations, the medium has had its share of disap-pointments and setbacks. Since the Web's beginnings, virtual reality has been touted as the answer to believers' prayers. With one eye on the spectacular popularity of so-called 'chat' groups among mainstream online service

[ gossip ]

● **Who's sorry now, Brad or Gwyn? The Awful Truth**

providers, and another on the seductive appeal of three-dimensional environments and personalized mascots to inhabit them, startups for these ephemeral 'worlds' proliferated, at least until recently, in a heady climate of venture capital investment. These companies quickly developed prototypes for applying virtual reality to the Web, yet so far the results have been mixed at best. The virtual reality market is at a 'virtual' standstill right now, a victim of the slower-than-hoped rate of adoption by consumers of sophisticated, super-powerful computers, and conflicting standards for VRML, the virtual reality modeling language. Yet the 'worlds' phenomenon, if the visionaries are correct, does seem to offer an engrossing model for the future interactivity of the Web, if only a business model can be found to implement it. **If at this** stage the Web is, to borrow a quip, "a medium that is rarely well done," it is also endlessly perfectible. As the computer goes from being a productivity tool to a tool for communication and fact-finding, the variety of experiences and activities online will exponentially increase. Who will design them? Engineers? Marketing types? Visual artists? More than likely, all three, although not always all three at any one time. As proficient designers learn to read the instructions, as conventional attitudes about what people want on the Web are dismantled, and as business clients learn that the graphic element of the Internet browser cannot be ignored, Web design will come into its own. Meanwhile the static, hierarchical organization of websites will give way to encroaching 'push' technology that streams updated information to the desktop and other innovations. Sometime not so far in the future, computers themselves will give way to new forms of hardware and software that further blur the distinction between the analog world of physical reality and the digital realm that's still being born. **None of** which will matter to you much one day when you're busily tending to that virtual pet of yours, some presently unimaginable creature that exists only in a fictitious, but infinitely alluring world.

**A worldwide
online community
of gay, lesbian, bi,
and trans people**

NETQUEERY
Everything
Queer
on the
Net

```
┌─────────────────────────────────────────────────────────────────────┐
│ ≡≡≡≡≡≡≡≡≡≡≡≡≡≡≡≡≡≡≡  Netscape: hind_site  ≡≡≡≡≡≡≡≡≡≡≡≡≡≡≡≡≡≡  │
├─────────────────────────────────────────────────────────────────────┤
│ Location: │ http://www.io360.com/v2/yo/look_harder/            │  ┌───┐ │
│                                                               │ │ N │ │
│ [What's New?] [What's Cool?] [Destinations] [Net Search] [People] [Software] │
├─────────────────────────────────────────────────────────────────────┤
│                                                                     │
│                                                                     │
│                                                                     │
│                                                                     │
│                              look harder                            │
│                                                                     │
│                                                                     │
│                                                                     │
│   exit                                                              │
│                                                                     │
│                                                                     │
└─────────────────────────────────────────────────────────────────────┘
```

Consultancies that provide creative services for the Web are subject to the same restrictions, frustrations and disappointments as traditional graphic design studios. Clients, already mystified by the design process, are flummoxed by the demands of new technology like the Internet: all too often, unfortunately, the same goes for the designers. People who design websites have produced a lot of work that makes more commercial sites pale by comparison. Why? Is it because the Web is such a new medium, or is it because that's the way it's always been – design studios doing their best work for themselves because, just perhaps, the design process is fundamentally flawed? For whatever reason, design studios' websites deliver much of the most compelling visual material on the Web. While many still cling to the 'electronic brochure' model, others are implementing the dynamics of the Web in a proof of process. The proof: we had to be much more selective with this section.

io360 http://www.io360.com i/o 360 digital design is a New York-based
design studio specializing in visual design in technology-mediated environments.
Its core staff of 20 designers and technologists strategize, conceptualize,
and implement a number of digital design projects – CD-ROM and IPK deveop-
ment, sites for the World Wide Web, corporate Intranet and Extranet
applications, as well as design research and development in emerging technology
arenas. Team Gong Szeto, Nam Szeto, Arkadiusz Banasik, Dindo Magallanes,
Creative Partners; Robert Clyatt, Managing Partner; Ralph Lucci, Senior Designer;
Sara Golding, Senior Designer; Monica Wong, Designer; Russell
Morgan, Design Technologist; Steve Kann, Lead Technologist/Administrator

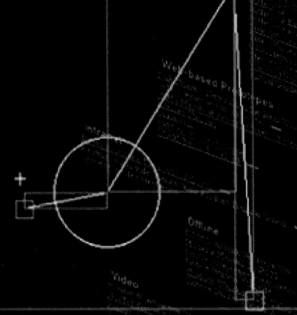

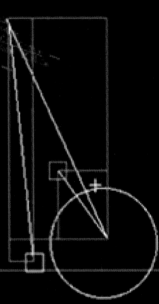

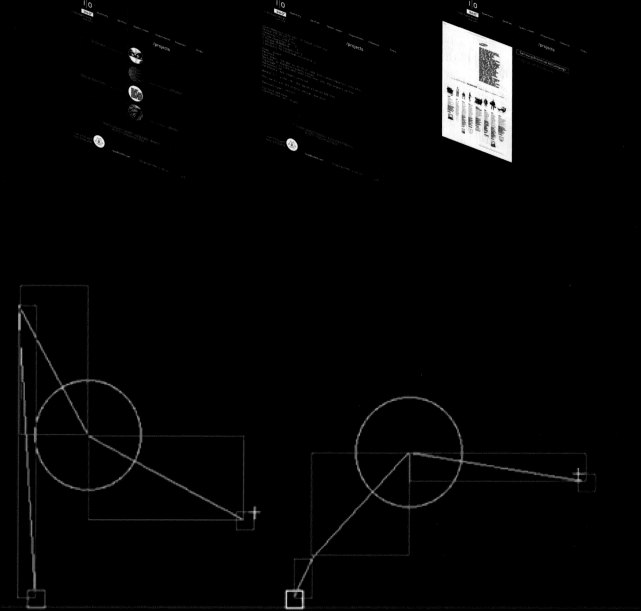

exit

22_

align window here

y0

01

02

03

04

05

06

07

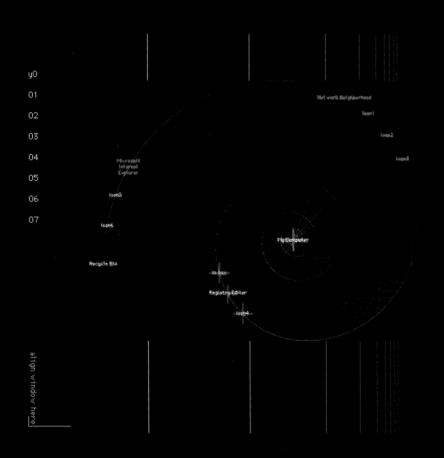

align window here

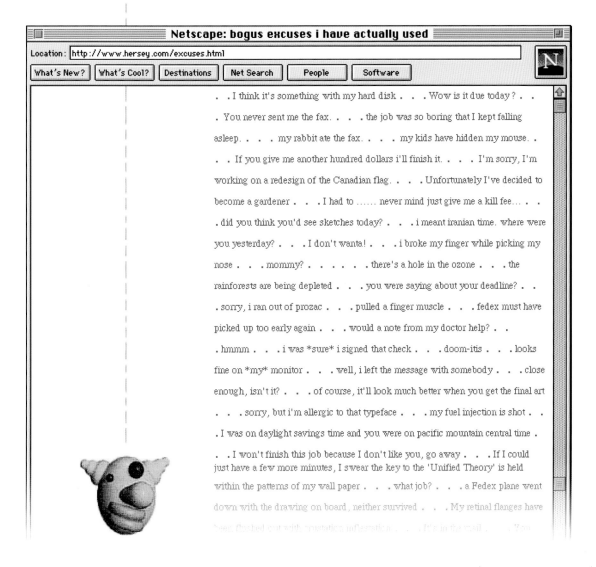

. . I think it's something with my hard disk . . . Wow is it due today ? . .
. You never sent me the fax . . . . the job was so boring that I kept falling
asleep . . . . my rabbit ate the fax . . . . my kids have hidden my mouse . .
. . If you give me another hundred dollars i'll finish it . . . . I'm sorry, I'm
working on a redesign of the Canadian flag . . . . Unfortunately I've decided to
become a gardener . . . I had to . . . . . . never mind just give me a kill fee . . . . .
. did you think you'd see sketches today? . . . i meant iranian time. where were
you yesterday? . . . I don't wanta! . . . i broke my finger while picking my
nose . . . mommy? . . . . . . there's a hole in the ozone . . . the
rainforests are being depleted . . . you were saying about your deadline? . .
. sorry, i ran out of prozac . . . pulled a finger muscle . . . fedex must have
picked up too early again . . . would a note from my doctor help? . .
. hmmm . . . i was *sure* i signed that check . . . doom-itis . . . looks
fine on *my* monitor . . . well, i left the message with somebody . . . close
enough, isn't it? . . . of course, it'll look much better when you get the final art
. . . sorry, but i'm allergic to that typeface . . . my fuel injection is shot . .
. I was on daylight savings time and you were on pacific mountain central time .
. . I won't finish this job because I don't like you, go away . . . If I could
just have a few more minutes, I swear the key to the 'Unified Theory' is held
within the patterns of my wall paper . . . what job? . . . . a Fedex plane went
down with the drawing on board, neither survived . . . My retinal flanges have
been flushed out with mutation infestation . . . . It's in the mail . . . . You

**John Hersey** http://www.hersey.com Self-described as "one guy's advanced primate
experiment," this diverting showcase for a leading digital illustrator uses
visual wit and self-deprecating humor to present the artist's eccentric graphic
inventions. Team John Hersey

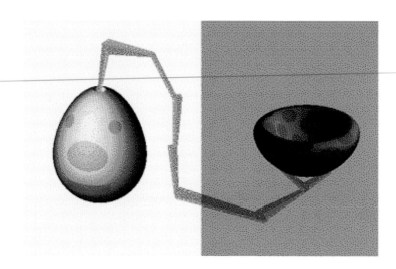

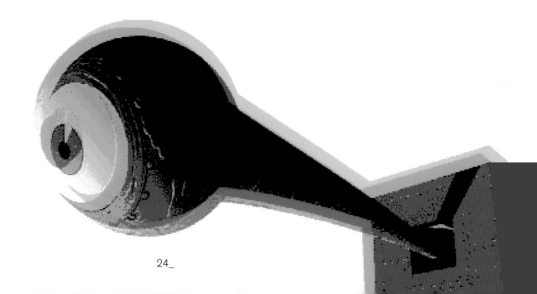

 "it rain"

[1)...<u>port</u>foolio]

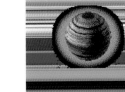

<u>1</u> | <u>2</u> | <u>3</u> | <u>4</u> | <u>5</u> | <u>6</u> | <u>7</u> | <u>8</u> | <u>9</u> | <u>10</u> | <u>11</u> | <u>12</u>
<u>13</u> | <u>14</u> | <u>15</u> | <u>16</u> | <u>17</u> | <u>18</u> | <u>19</u> | <u>20</u> | <u>21</u> | <u>22</u> | <u>23</u> | <u>24</u>

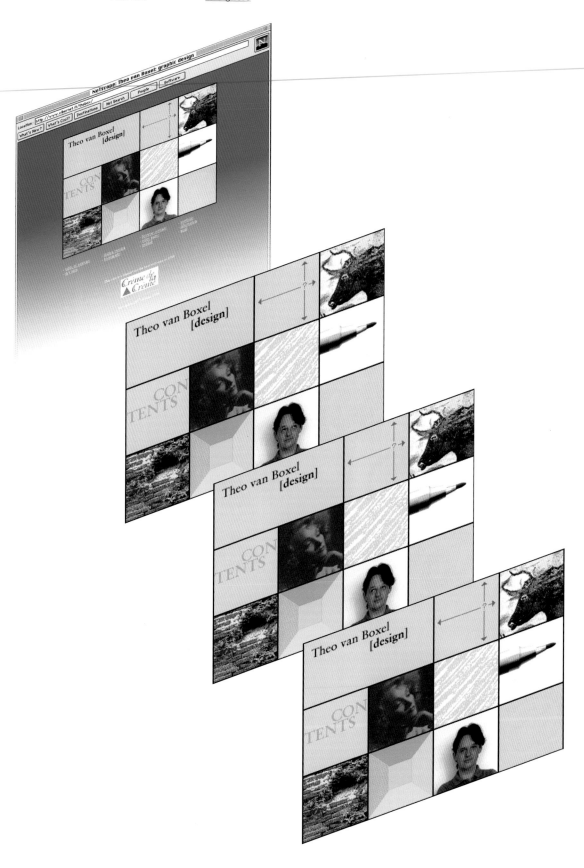

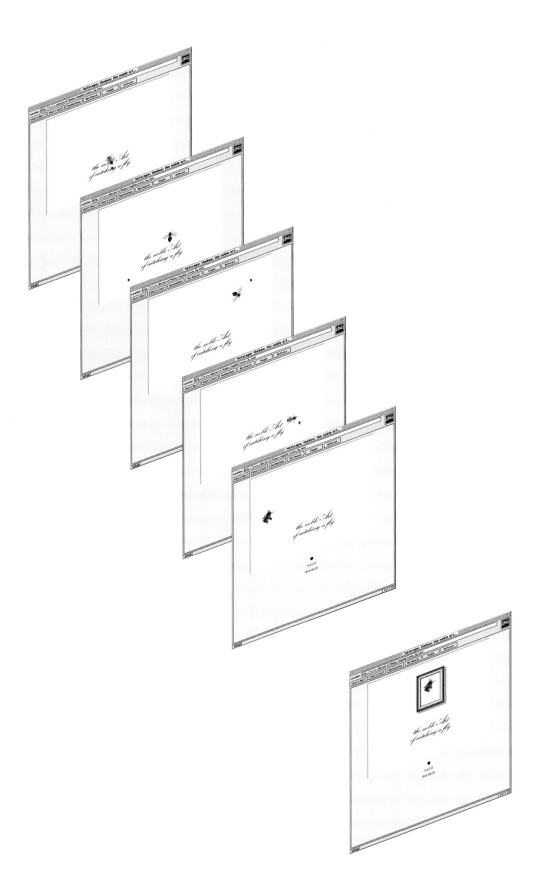

**Studio Grafico Theo van Boxel** http://www.cibernet.it/thebox
Promotional material, graphic and interactive designs. Studio Studio Grafico
Theo van Boxel Team Theo van Boxel

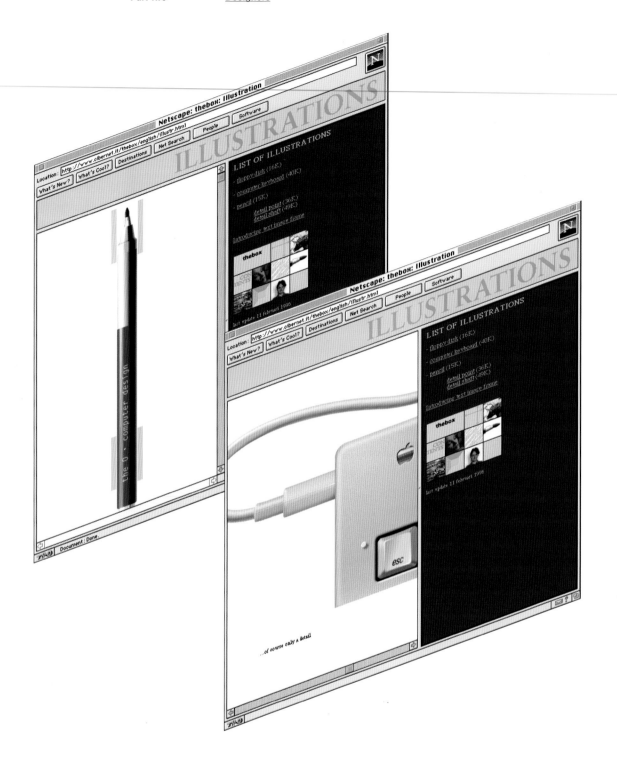

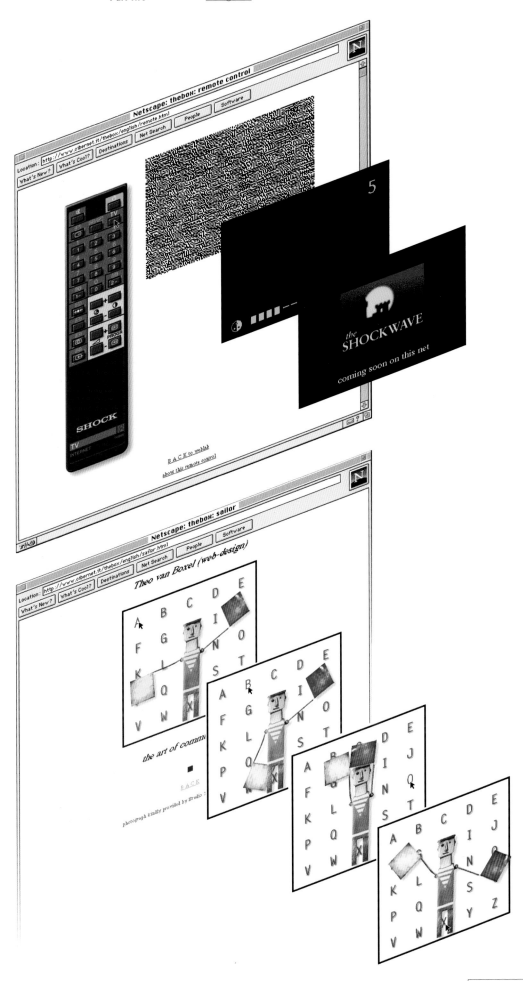

**Post Tv** http://www.posttv.com Post Tv is a 'virtual sandbox' of original entertainment
formatted for the Internet. Characterized by reckless experimentation with
the latest advances in Web technology, the site includes features like Playpage,
Canned Bland, Bedtime Stories, Post News and Homing. **Studio** Post Tool
design **Team** David Karam, Producer, Designer, Illustrator, Webmasta; Gigi Biederman,
Designer, Illustrator; Tom Bland, Producer, Sound Designer, Stella Lai,
Designer, Illustrator

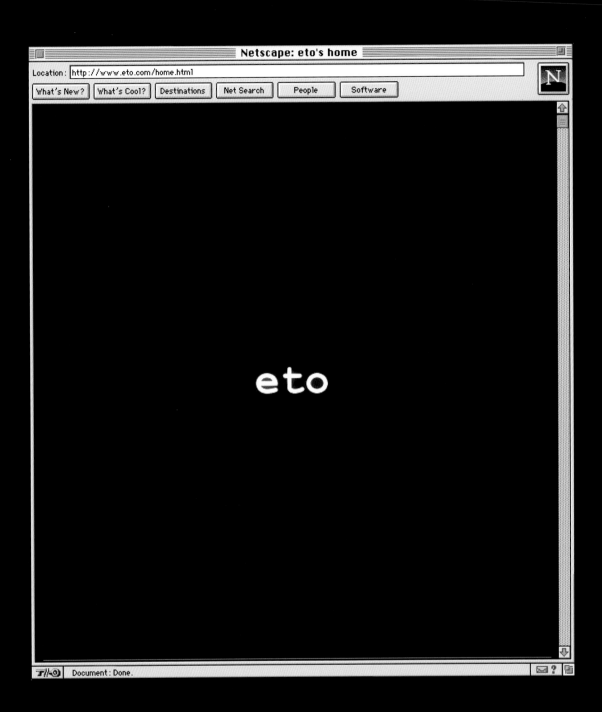

Kouichirou Eto http://eto.com A catalog of this designer's work.
Studio Kouichirou Eto @ Tokyo, Japan Team Kouichirou Eto

c o n t a c t

**DotPaint**

**PeepHole**

**text works**

**How to use
CGI and Form**
*In Japanese*

**essay about
Interface**
*In Japanese*

**essay about
Information Space**
*In Japanese*

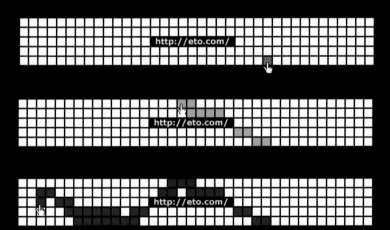

http://eto.com/

http://eto.com/

http://eto.com/

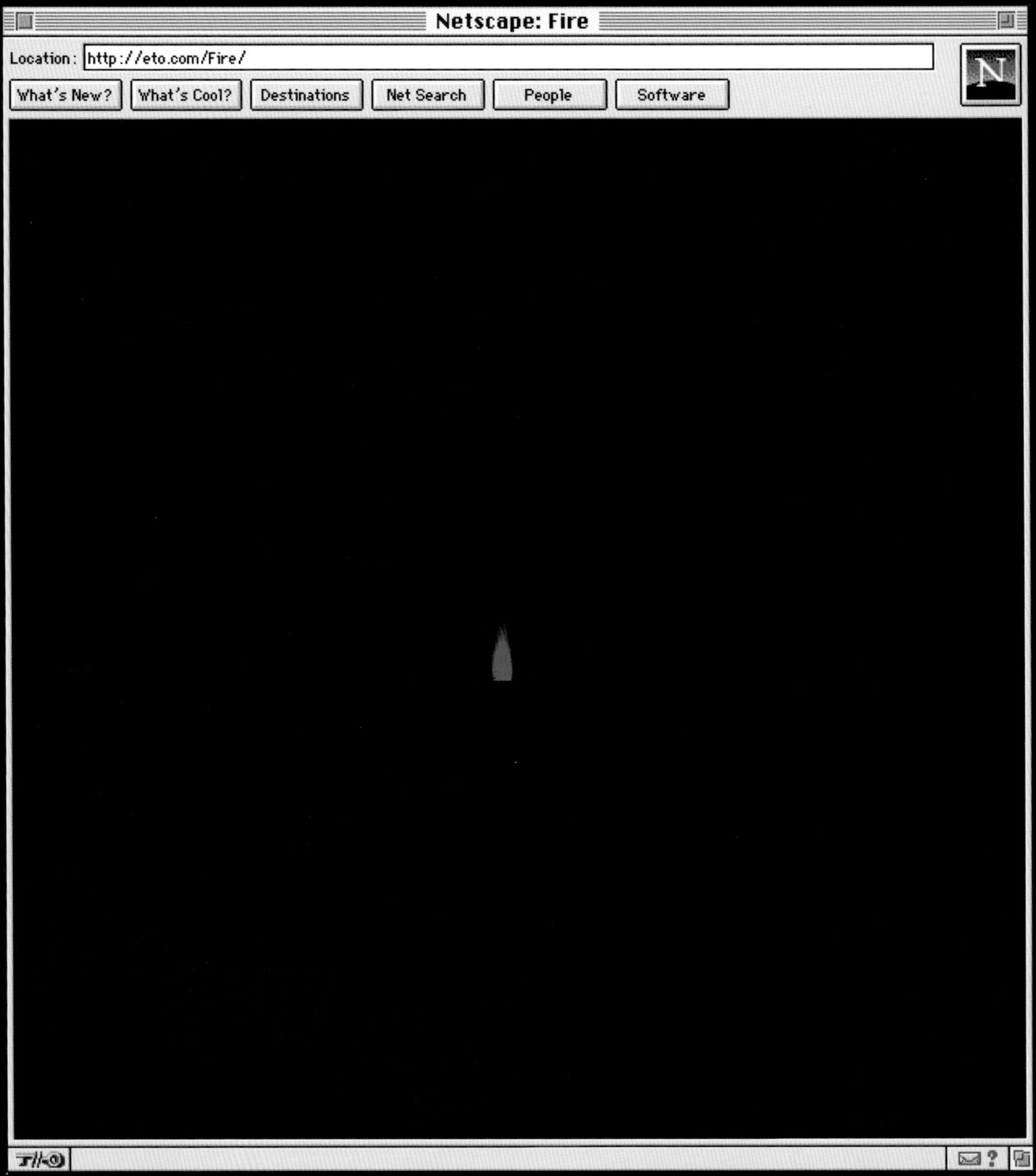
Netscape: Fire
Location: http://eto.com/Fire/
What's New?
What's Cool?
Destinations
Net Search
People
Software

Jlc Netscape - [essay about Interface]

ファイル(F)  編集(E)  表示(V)  ジャンプ(G)  ブックマーク(B)  オプション(O)  ディレクトリ(D)  ウィンドウ(W)  ヘルプ(H)

場所: **http://eto.com/iface/**

コンピューターにおける
無制限の
有限について

Author: 江渡 浩一郎

コンピューターを使うことにどのような意味があるのかということ を絵画とコンピューターグラフィックの関係を例にとって考えてみる。

コンピューターを使って絵を作る。これはいわゆるコンピューター グラフィックス(以下CGと略す。)というものだ。僕は大学に入って、はじめて本格的にCGというものにふれた。それ以前はちょっとプロ グラムをかいて、画面になにか絵を出した程度で、CGがどういう意 味をもっているのかは考えていなかった。

大学で習った**CG**というのはこのようなものだった。まず、**shell** と いう簡単な言語のようなものを使って、どのような形を作るのかを書く。それをプログラムにわたし、コンピューターに絵を描いても らう。このとき、絵を描いてもらうのに、命令を言葉であたえるというところが非常におもしろかった。同時に非常に奇妙な感じもし た。ちょうど絵と言葉との間に一対一の対応関係がなりたってしま

文書: 完了。

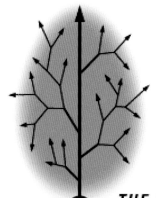

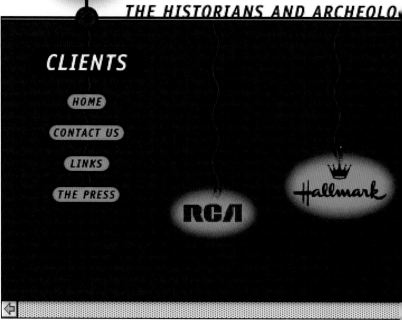

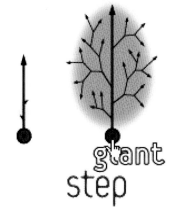

**Giant Step** http://www.giantstep.com Team Kerry O'Donnel, Programmer;
Xavier Wynn, Sean Moran, Sheau Hui Ching, Designers.

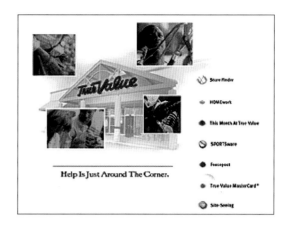

TS WILL ONE DAY DISCOVER THAT THE ADS OF OUR TIMES ARE THE RICHEST

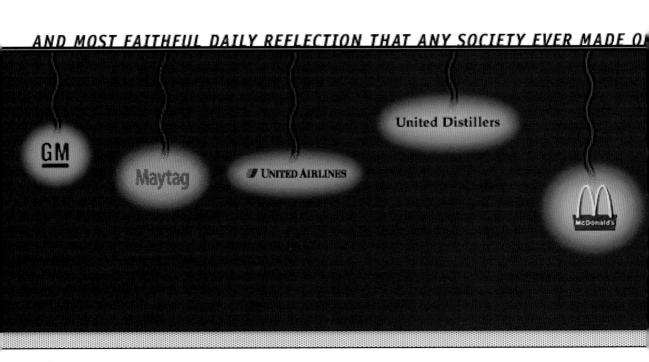

AND MOST FAITHFUL DAILY REFLECTION THAT ANY SOCIETY EVER MADE O

'TS ENTIRE RANGE OF ACTIVITIES – MARSHALL MCLUHAN

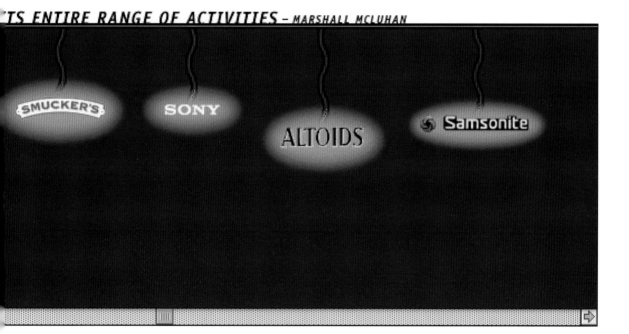

Higher

The Whimsyload http://www.whimseyload.com The Whimsyload is a 'showcase of wonder' featuring the delightfully offbeat work of New York-based artist Rodney Alan Greenblat. The site is home to a gallery of original art, an entertainment center, a children's book zone, a portfolio of commercial work, music demos, and just plain weird experimental digital pieces called the Creative Rodney Art Projects (CRAP). Studio The Center for Advanced Whimsy Team Rodney Alan Greenblat, Director; Jenny Horn, Graphics; Deena Lebow, Manager

mp.html

Stop

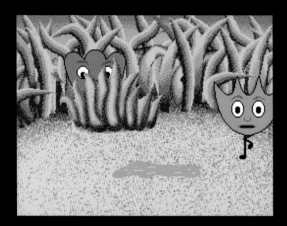 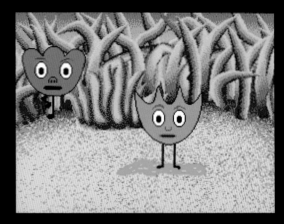

As it is common knowledge at this point, The Tooli Bugs reside on little sandy island jetties of the great Tube Grass Marsh. The name 'bugs' is misleading. These creatures walk upright on two legs, but have no other appendages on their bodies. The name 'Tooli' comes from their beautiful call, which sounds to us like a nasal child hooting "tooli, tooli."

The reclusive Spotted Thorn Bunnies inhabit the darkest and most dangerous part of Prickerbush Valley. Surrounded by dense foliage and razor sharp thorns, their lives are spent darting through the underbrush in search of their favorite food, Tar Gum Nuts. Because their fur is hardened into knife like pointed barbs, physical contact with these bunnies is

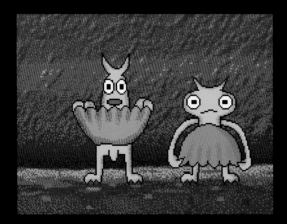 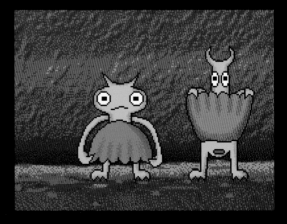

The curious little Arachnopants live in the deep cracks of Buttgrin Canyon. The males and females are identical until they lift the skirt-like flap of loose skin that surrounds the abdomen. In this way they display, and announce their intentions.

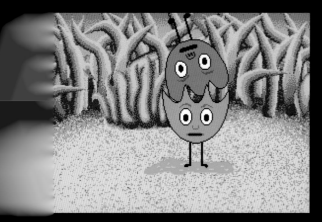
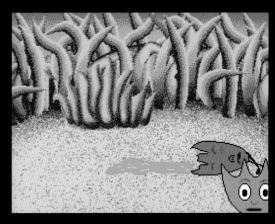

Although the males do trap the females and fertilize them against their will, the females get their revenge. Neglected n the first version of this presentation the females deliberately kick and bite the exhausted males in the head, often causing sever mental damage. Few male Toolies mate twice, and the ones that do generally proceed with great caution.

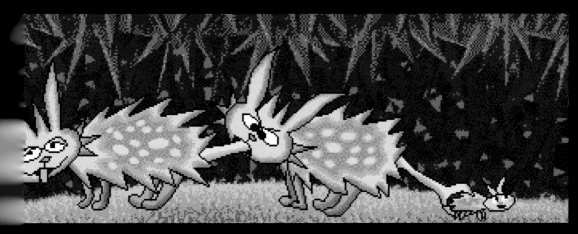

mpossible without injury. When mating this could cause a problem, but evolution has solved this impediment. Their leshy tails, the only area not covered with spines, acts as male appendage and female birth tube. Thorn Bunnies have no jestation period. Pups are instantly produced seconds after fertilization.

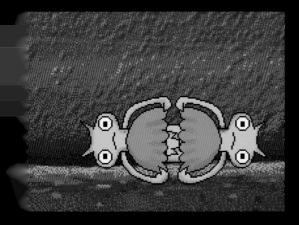
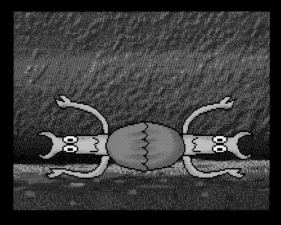

Arachnopants are plentiful in the canyon, often moving in large herds from place to place to feed. They are generally happy little creatures, and the young often participate in games, including 'roll-the-rock' and 'squirt-cold-water-up-your-brothers-skirt.'

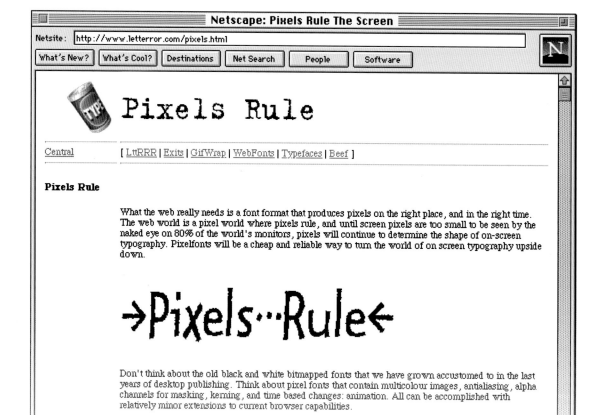

**LettError Type & Typography** http://www.letterror.com The site features presentations of the designers' ideas on type and typography, and their opinions on various matters concerning type, fonts, and the Web. Descriptions of LettError projects such as the various typefaces, tools such as BitPull, and lately, the GifWrap Webfont utility are included. **Team** Erik van Blokland, Just van Rossum, Designers, Programmers, Illustrators, Type Designers, Writers

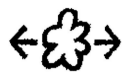

be used in smaller sizes without losing much clarity. Making the font larger will of course show the pixels.

Time based information can be added as well. As currently on display on this page with animated gifs.

Pixelfonts can be used as an efficient way to store frequently used images as buttons, icons and other 'structural' graphics.

If the rendered size increases, compression increases as well.

**What should be done**

Obviously, this is not a detailed plan on how to implement pixel fonts. I want to prove that these fonts have a place on the web, and that it is possible to use them and make them with a reasonable amount of work.

Pixelfonts do not replace outline fonts, but they provide a way to use typography on webpages without embedding of outlines, a choice that should be available to all users and authors. Pixelfonts do not have to answer to all situations, but they offer a couple of exciting possibilities in return, also something that should be available to the web world. Pixelfonts will decrease the risk of illegal use of outline fonts. People cannot steal what is not there. There will continue to be a market for typefaces, as web authors can include pixelfont versions of new outline fonts without breaking their license agreements. Even as pixel fonts can be rendered automatically from outline fonts, it is also a way to experiment with animated type, colourful type, i.e. the things outline fonts cannot reach. Tools to create pixel fonts are simple.

None of the ideas listed above is actually shockingly new, some of them are not even original. As a type designer and a web author I am aware of the risks of embedding outline fonts in webpages, but I also long for better typographic capabilities for webpages. I believe that pixel fonts can be a solution to both, and deserves a chance to be investigated.

Links to web font experiments

- Paul Haeberli's web font proposal. It's all there.
- Stop looking, GifWrap is here.

---

Central      [ LttRRR | Exits | GifWrap | WebFonts | Typefaces | Beef ]

© LettError

R/GA DIGITAL STUDIOS

**R/GA INTERACTIVE**  **COMPANY**

**FUN**  **R/GA PRINT**

**R/GREENBERG ASSOCIATES**

OLDSMOBILE

RiGA
INTERACTIVE

◀GOLDENEYE

RiGREENBERG
ASSOCIATES

◀INTEL

BACK

RiGA
PRINT

◀JOHN
HANCOCK

MORE

ARCHIVES

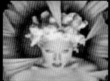

◀MADONNA

R/GA Digital Studios http://www.rga.com The site is inspired by the idea
of an 'information machine' that reconfigures itself based on the user's choices.
It works outside of the spatial metaphor implicit in most Web navigation.
Users are not 'going' to places or pages, instead information is 'coming' to them.
Visual and structural design reinforce this concept. The entire site is
displayed within a 16-rectangle grid-like layout. Text and pictures appear and
disappear within these fixed locations, as though information were passing
through a container. Individual content areas are illustrated by elements chosen
on-the-fly from a larger database of potential choices. In some sections,
display is random. The sense of streaming information is also heightened by
animation of the rectangles during downloads. Team Alicia Vance,
Producer; Karen Sideman, Creative Director; Scott Prindle, Programmer;
Eleanor Tsang, Webmaster

pan
UP

TURNER CLASSIC MOVIES
'Director of the Month'
© 1994 Turner Entertainment
Designed and produced by R.G.A./L.A

The main titles reflect title design and
animation from the Golden Age of film.
The beat and rhythm found in the
composition are inspired by 1950s
and 60s classic jazz album covers.

I need a YELLOW GEL

roll 'em!

TCM

**NETWITS**

NETWITS
Produced by R/GA-Interactive and
The Microsoft Network

NetWits is an interactive game show,
replete with a dashing host and great
prizes. NetWits draws together
thousands of contestants from all
walks of life into multi-player games
where everyone has a chance to win

# cronan design | strategy + design

**Cronan Design** http://www.cronan.com Cronan Design is a firm specializing
in visual communications: corporate identity and communications, product
development, packaging, marketing communications and visual merchandising.
In support of strategic marketing initiatives, the studio provides consulting
services in the following areas: communications planning, product planning,
program management, and organizational development, in the belief that
the impact of visual communications products is highly dependent on the organizational context in which they are executed. Team Michael Cronan,
Creative Director; Anthony Yell, Senior Designer; Joseph Stitzlein, Designer

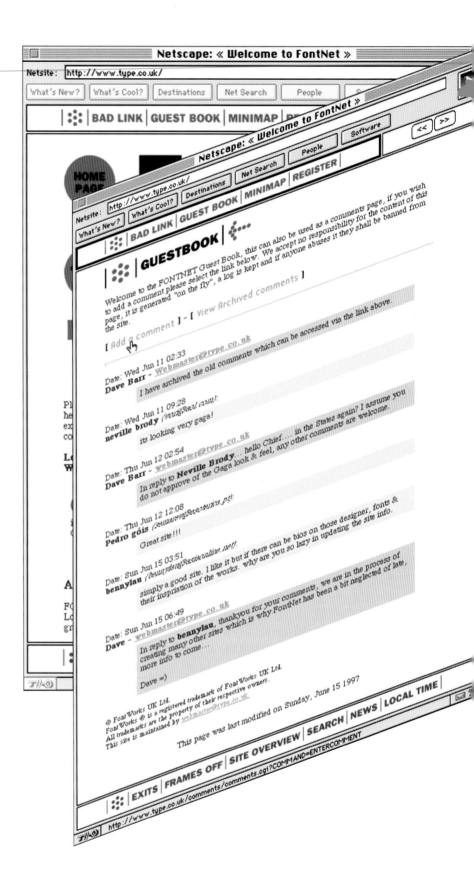

**FontNet** http://www.type.co.uk Client FontWorks UK Ltd Studio FontWorks
Font design, typography, related issues. Team Stuart Jensen, Managing
Director; Neville Brody, Creative Director; Mike Williams, Simon Staines,
Designers; Dave Barr, Webmaster; Steve Miller, Marketing

54_

deejean@indy.net

Entropy8 http://www.entropy8.com Studio Entropy8 Digital Arts
Team Auriea Harvey, Artist, Designer, Webmistress, Programmer

Be Strong
Be Strong
Be STRONG

**(Untitled)**

Be it always that your eyes are. . .
Be it always that your lips are. . .
Be it always that your arms are. . .
Be it always that your arms are. . .

Be it always that your love is. . .
Be it always that your faith is. . .
Be it always that your strength is. . .
Be it always that your mind is. . .

If I could find the words to finish the phrase It would still not be you

**Searching**

As I sit I wonder why
Why oh why cant I cry

You are not around
You are not around
You are simply not here

These feelings, how they call
Cut through me, soul and all

Where are you?
Where are you?
Where have you been?

**Completed**

Im finished
Im done
Now the moment has come
The moment where the end of it is.
Im not depressed
Im not sad
Just done.

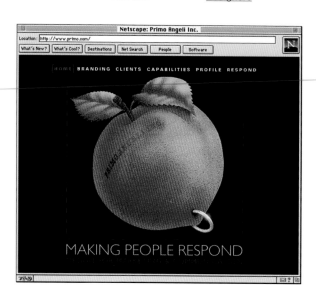

**THE RIGHT NAME. THE RIGHT RESPONSE.**

**Primo Angeli** <u>http://www.primo.com</u> Primo Angeli has built an international reputation in the field of graphic communications, especially packaging, corporate identity, and environmental graphics. The studio's client list includes Coca-Cola, Nestlé, Visa, Hunt-Wesson, Kraft General Foods, General Mills, Crystal Geyser, Brown-Forman, Miller Brewing, Quaker Oats Company, Shaklee Corporation, Hyatt Hotels Corporation, G. Heileman Brewing Company, Henry Weinhard, DHL Worldwide Express, Christian Brothers Winery, Bank of America, Wells Fargo Bank, AT&T, Banana Republic, Levi Strauss, Philippine Airlines, the Oakland A's, the San Francisco International Airport, Xerox Corporation, The Asian Art Museum, and Guinness. Team Primo Angeli, Creative Director; Brody Hartman, Art Director; Sara Sandstrom and Ryan Medeiros, Designers; Jean Galeazzi, Copy Writer; Ryan Medeiros, Webmaster

ICON OR CON MAN?

**Mismatch.**

TASTE A PEEL?

contact
projects
bios

map
search
links
world
tool
stratu
perihelio
forum

karl
guestboo

|------------05/97-|  |------------04/97-|  |------------02/97-|  |------------02/97-|  |------------01/97-|

**netscape**          **collegenet**        **microsoft vrml**      **crutch**          **dive bar**
html                  vrml 2.0              html, vrml 2.0         html, vrml 2.0      vrml 2.0, multi-user
/pmedium scale        medium scale         medium scale           medium scale        small scale

Construct Internet Design http://www.construct.net Construct is an Internet
design company that builds immersive online experiences. The studio
offers technical, design, and conceptual expertise through the innovative
combination of HTML, VRML, Java, MUDs, C and C++ coding; genetic
algorithms and other experimental programming techniques; and traditional
design practices of illustration, architecture, modeling, page layout,
typography, writing, and painting. Construct also conducts research in the
areas of digital transactions and commerce, agents, bots and artificial
life. Team Annette Loudon, Webmistress; Michael Gough, Creative Director;
Mark Meadows, Chief Investigating Officer; stnkfoot, Stunt Designer;
Cynsa Borranis, Web Engineer; Gabriella Marks, Texter

| s rio project | vrm197 | stratus | euclid | sgi's oobe | bigbook | srl |
|---|---|---|---|---|---|---|
| l 2.0, graphics | vrml 2.0, graphics | html, vrml 1.0 | vrml 1.0, html | html, vrml 2.0 | vrml 1.0 | html |
| large scale | small scale | large scale | medium scale | large scale | large scale | medium scale |

|------------10/95-| |------------09/95-| |------------09/95-| |------------08/95-| |------------06/95-|

   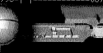 

<u>cyberspazio</u>          <u>pacbell</u>          <u>the rift</u>          <u>sgi</u>          <u>tierra</u>
  vrml 1.0                 html                  vrml 1.0               vrml 1.0              vrml 1.0
medium scale          medium scale          large scale          small scale          medium scale

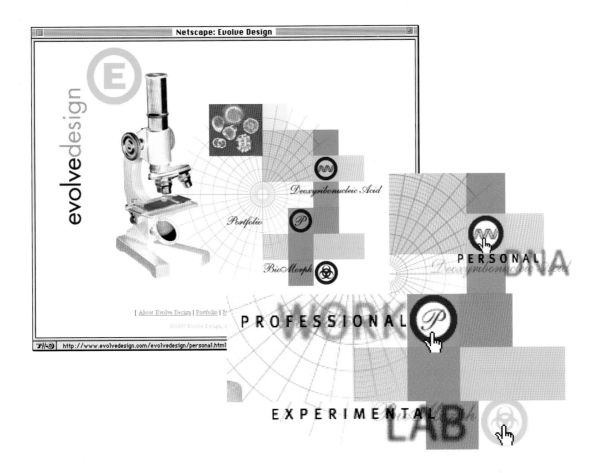

**Evolve Design** http://www.evolvedesign.com The site includes a portfolio and
statement of design strategy for the sudio, and personal information
about designer Marc Wilcox including a resume and a design gallery of ideas
and imagery. **Studio** Evolve Design **Team** Marc Wilcox

Razorfish http://www.razorfish.com Razorfish, Inc. is a strategic digital communications firm based in New York City. Known for its award-winning design, original content and technology, the firm works across platforms including the World Wide Web, CD-ROM, broadband networks, gaming platforms, online services, and broadcast. Razorfish clients include IBM, America Online, Time Warner, AT&T, Sony, and Ralph Lauren.Team Thomas Mueller, Lead Designer; Marc Tinkler, Senior Technologist/Designer; Oz Lubling, Senior Technologist; Michael Chu, Designer; Melinda Fletcher, Production Specialist; Becky Carpenter, Project Manager; Peter Mattei, Senior Writer; Neith Preston, Quality Assurance Specialist; Michael Freedman, Mary Azzart, Writers; Jose Caballer, Designer; Alex Clifton, Artist/Production Specialist; Craig M. Kanarick, Creative Director; Jeff Dachis, Executive Producer

**fontBoy** http://www.well.com/user/bobauf/fontboy.html An online catalog of
the fontBoy library of fonts. **Studio** Aufuldish & Warinner **Team** Bob
Aufuldish, Design Director, Designer, Webmaster; Bob Aufuldish, Kathy Warinner,
Font Designers; Mark Bartlett, Writer, Editor

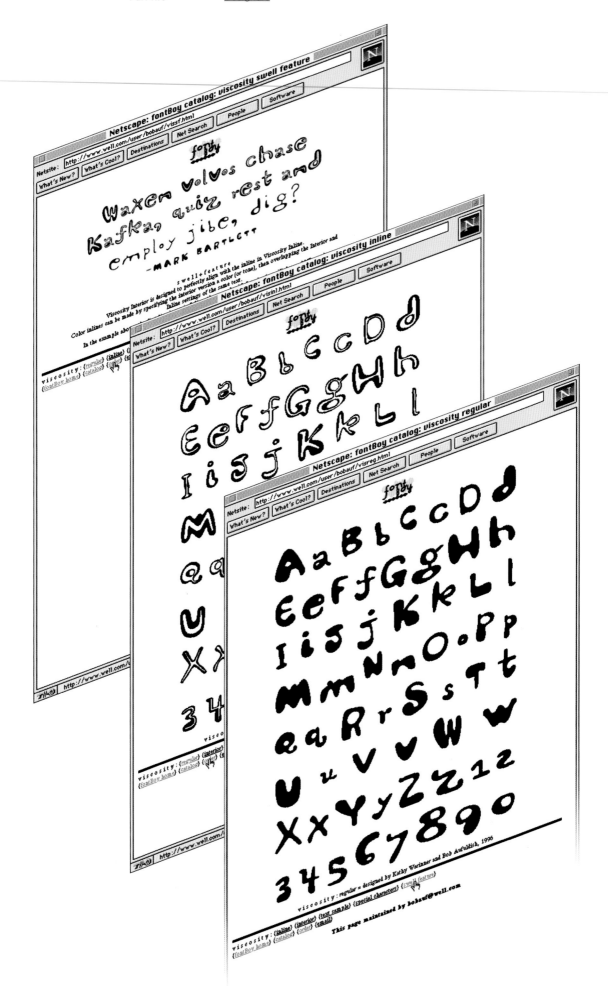

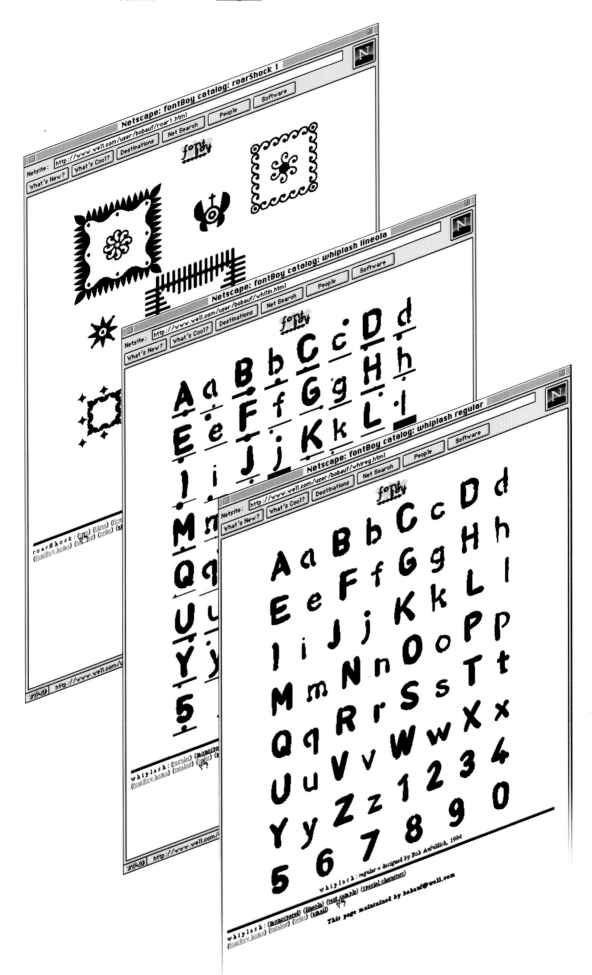

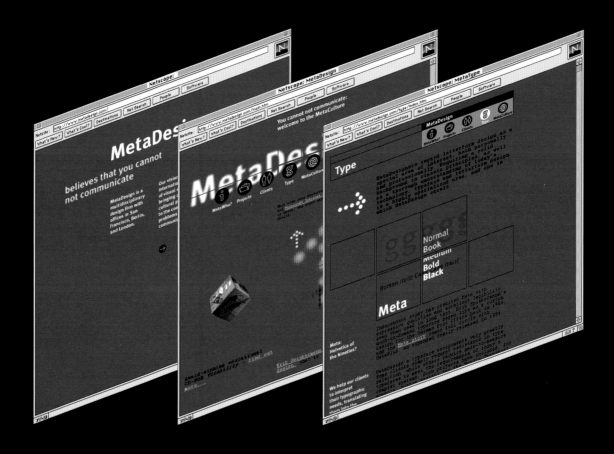

http://www.metadesign.com MetaDesign is a multidisciplinary
design firm with offices in Berlin, London and San Francisco. Founded in the
early 1980's by noted letterform/graphic designer Erik Spiekermann, the firm
has grown into a combined staff of over 100 designers, strategic planners
and implementation specialists. The studio's site offers marketing and
recruitment material, incorporating background information about MetaDesign, its
clients, projects, and philosophy. **Team** Bill Hill and Terry Irwin, Principals;
Rick Lowe, Creative Director; Kevin Farnham, Webmaster; Joseph Ternes,
Programming and Production

Netscape: MetaWho?

Netsite: http://www.metadesign.com/metawho/index.htm

What's New?   What's Cool?   Destinations   Net Search   People   Software

MetaDesign

# MetaWho?     MetaWho? Projects Clients Type MetaCulture

**MetaDesign** is a multidisciplinary design firm with offices in San Francisco, Berlin, and London, with a combined staff of over 160 designers, **technologists**, planners and implementation **specialists**. We believe that design is first and foremost an intellectual process: we like to think about our projects before we decide how they're going to look. But we also know that to communicate an idea we need to give it an exciting and innovative **visual language**.

**MetaDesign is a multidisciplinary design firm with offices in San Francisco, Berlin, and London.**

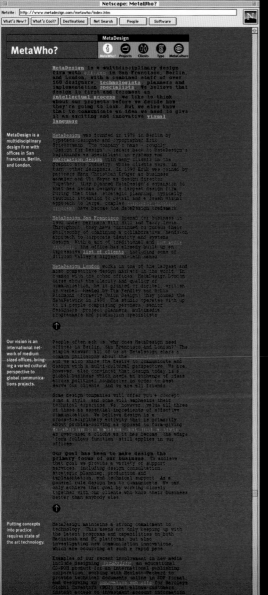

MetaDesign was founded in 1979 in Berlin by typeface designer and typographer Erik Spiekermann. The company's name — roughly "Design for Design" — harks back to MetaDesign's beginnings as specialist in systems and information design. With many clients in the graphic arts industry, whose clients were, in turn, other designers. In 1990 Erik was joined by partners Hans Christian Krüger as business manager and Uli Mayer as design director. Together, they planned MetaDesign's expansion to what has become Germany's largest design firm. During that time, strategic planning, typically fanatic attention to detail and a fresh visual approach to large, complex ...... ......... have become the MetaDesign trademark.

MetaDesign San Francisco opened for business in 1992 under partners Bill Hill and Terry Irwin. Throughout, they have continued to pursue their philosophy of combining a collaborative hands-on approach to corporate identity and systems design. With a mix of traditional and .... ....... ......., the office has already built up an impressive list of clients, including some of Silicon Valley's biggest ... well-known names.

MetaDesign London works in one of the largest and most competitive design markets in the world. In common with the other offices, MetaDesign London cares about the clarity and quality of communication, be it printed or digital, written or verbal. Headed by Tim Fendley and Robin Richmond (formerly Union Design) they joined the MetaNetwork in 1995. The studio operates with up to 15 people comprising partners, senior designers, project planners, multimedia programmers and production specialists.

**Our vision is an international network of medium-sized offices, bringing a varied cultural perspective to global communications projects.**

People often ask us "why does MetaDesign need offices in Berlin, San Francisco and London?" The simple answer: all of us at MetaDesign share a common philosophy about the ... ... ... and we also share the desire to communicate and design with a multi-cultural perspective. We are, however, also convinced that design today is a global business which needs an exchange of ideas across political boundaries in order to best serve our clients. And we are all friends.

Some design companies will offer you a concept and a style, and some will emphasize their technical expertise. We, however, value all three of these as essential ingredients of effective communication. We believe design is a cross-disciplinary activity that is primarily about problem-solving as opposed to form-giving. Or ... design is a method, but just a style. As over-used a cliché as it has become, the adage "form follows function" still applies in our offices.

**Our goal has been to make design the primary focus of our business.** To achieve that goal we provide a variety of support services, including design consultation, strategic planning, production and implementation, and technical support. As a general rule design has to communicate. We can only achieve that goal by working closely together with our clients who know their business better than anybody else.

**Putting concepts into practice requires state of the art technology.**

MetaDesign maintains a strong commitment to technology. This means not only keeping up with the latest programs and capabilities on both Macintosh and PC platforms, but also investigating new communication innovations, which are occurring at such a rapid pace.

Examples of our recent involvement in new media include designing *MetaTalk*, an educational CD-ROM product for an international publishing corporation, working with Hewlett-Packard to provide technical documents online in PDF format, and designing an *interactive web-site* for Barclays Global Investors (BGI) that allows customers instant access to investment account information.

**All MetaDesigners share a love of, and a commitment to, the highest level of typography.**

At MetaDesign, we believe in bringing our ............ ... ... ... ... ...

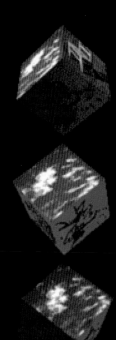

MetaDesign Berlin/San Francisco/London are measured against the First Axiom of Communication: You cannot not communicate.

## San Francisco

**MetaDesign**
350 Pacific Avenue, 3rd floor
San Francisco, CA 94111
Tel (415) 627 0790
Fax (415) 627 0795

From its start in a small office with a staff of
three in 1992, MetaDesign San Francisco now
employs 30 designers and support personnel, with
a team of six consultants who work on special
assignments.

More business meant taking on more staff, which
in turn required more space. In December 1994 we
moved from Broadway to a building at the corner
of Pacific Avenue and Battery in downtown San
Francisco, where we now occupy 7,800 square feet
of studio space.

Together, we have over 70 years of collective
experience in designing, managing and
implementing identities for major corporations,
combined with extensive exposure to digital media
to service many high-tech clients, including
Adobe Systems, IBM, Tandem and Apple Computer.

Current San Francisco MetaDesigners and
staff are Nike Abbink, John Clise, Kaare Fallon,
Kevin Farnham, Hillary Geller, Kimberlee Maggie,
Marissa Maresco, Bill Hill, Terry Irwin, Rick
Lowe, Kelly Irish, Elizabeth Jones, Conor Mangat,
Pilar Manjarrez, Natalie Maric, Christopher
Myers, Patrick Newbery, David Hong, Kay
Nothstein, Ellie Oh, Shel Perkins, Joseph Ternes,
Stephanie Tripier, Eva Walter, Anne Warhol and
Jya Warhol

## Berlin

**MetaDesign**
Bergmannstrasse 102
D-10961 Berlin
Tel (030) 69 57 92-00
Fax (030) 69 57 92-22

MetaDesign Berlin opened its doors in 1990,
somewhat ironically on Potsdamer Platz – right by
the Berlin Wall – and just as the monument to the
Cold War began to be pulled down. A rebirth of
earlier MetaDesign incarnations (Mark 1, '79–'83
and Mark 2, '84–'89), it grew swiftly under the
leadership of Erik Spiekermann, Hans Christian
Krüger, and Uli Mayer.

In 1991 we moved to our present location at
Bergmannstraße, where we now occupy three floors
of a large industrial unit. MetaDesign in Berlin
consists of two legally separated companies, the
design firm MetaDesign and the pre-press company
CitySats, which MetaDesign acquired in 1992. Both
companies work together fully integrated and at
present employ a staff of about 120, thereby
making it the largest company of its kind in
Germany. Together we offer a wide range of
services: corporate design, typography, 3-D
design, new media design, production,
typesetting, reprographics, film output and many
more

The present long-term client list consists of
some major German companies like Audi, Boehringer
Pharmaceuticals and VW. Also well known is Meta's
work in the field of public transportation, for
example BVG and Düsseldorf Airport.

Current Berlin MetaDesigners are Rayan
Abdullah, Petra Arndt, HOL Barr, Pia Betton,
Stefan K. Bischoff, Dieter Bldöße, Michael Boeck,
Beate Brauner, Richard Buhl, Cornelia Brüning,
Theartje van Caspel, Gerald Christ, Ulrike Deam,
Claudia Dracksträtter, Claus Drueppel, Chris
Eisenkolb, Harry Enke, Asharna Fischer, Charly
Frech, Heide Frey, Isolde Frey, Michel Gabriel,
Axel Gries, Lucas de Groot, Sylvia Heim, Andreas
Haresdorff, Brigitte Hartwig, Karsten Henze, Colin
Huntley, Britta Jaensch, Christiaan von Zampta,
Andrea Keil, Jörn König, Freyja Enk, Axel
Kelaschnik, Hannes Krüger, Rosa Löffel, Nadja
Lorenz, Uli Mayer, Anne Mertini, Ulli Okryork,
Roland Metzler, Eva Nagl, Matthias Opitz, Stephan
Platz, Katrin Randel, Sylvia Robeck, Fabien
Rottke, Jin Rudolf, Silvie Rüstler, Ole Schäfer,
Kai Schnitter, Bruno Schmidt, Oliver
Schmiedhals, Holger Schmirgalski, Barbara Scholz
Marianna Schuler, Susanne Schulz, Buckie
Schuppenhauer, Andy Siegel, Erik Spiekermann,
Carolyn Steinbeck, Robert Stulle, Brian Switzer,
Roberta de Wilhena Rees, Marion Walsdorff,
Dorothee Wainlich, Frank Westermann and Michael
Winn

## London

**MetaDesign**
71 Leonard Street
London EC2A 4QS
Tel (0171) 613 5558
Fax (0171) 613 5499

MetaDesign London (formerly Union Design) was
formed in 1991 and incorporated into MetaDesign in
1995. The senior partners are Tim Fendley and Robin
Richmond. The office now houses a team of up to 14
people ranging from support personnel to multimedia
programmers, production specialists and writers.
MetaDesign London work with clients across a broad
range of industries such as publishing, banking,
furniture design, stock libraries, multimedia firms
and the voluntary sector. Based in Shoreditch on
the fringes of the City of London, the team
monitors the latest developments in digital
technology to ensure that briefs are answered in
the most appropriate way.

Current London MetaDesigners are: Andy Tough
Ben Teppenden, Robin Richmond, Gail Mellows,
Valentin Hindermann, Nette Heinz, Andreas Harding,
Tim Fendley, Sam Davy, John Crawford and Patrick
Eagles

**M.A.D.** http://www.madxs.com M.A.D. cofounder Erik Adigard is a regular contributor to the opening pages of Wired and, with his partner Patricia McShane, has produced critically accalimed visual communications for a variety of clients. The site serves as both a portfolio of work and a sample of the studio's problem-solving capabilities, given the limitations of website creation tools at the time. Team Patricia McShane, Designer, Webmaster; Patricia McShane, Erik Adigard, Illustrators

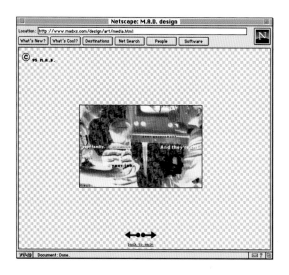

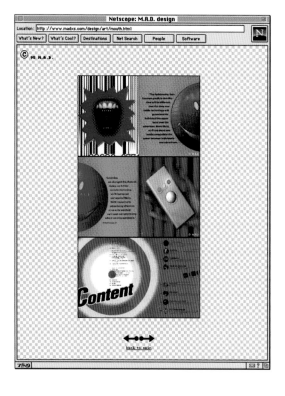

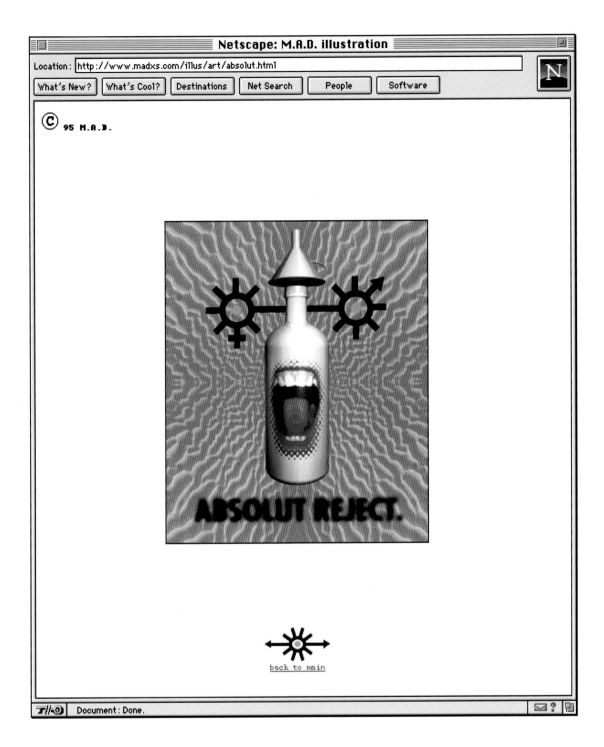

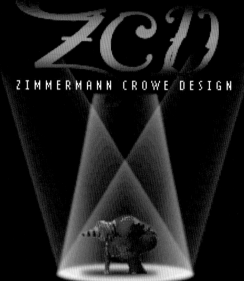

ABOUT ZCD          PORTFOLIO          SITE MAP

Zimmermann Crowe Design http://www.zcd.com Zimmermann Crowe Design
is a full-service graphic design firm which offers its clients communication
planning, project management and design and production services. Specialties
include retail enviromental design, typography for film and video, and
corporate identity systems and communications. Team Dennis Crowe, Creative
Director; Roger Wong, Webmaster; Roger Wong, Dennis Crowe, Designers;
Dennis Crowe, Neal Zimmermann, Editor; Tiffany Smith, HTML Programmer;
Silicon Reef, High-end Java Script Programming and Website Host

LEVI'S VIDEOS
MTV TOP OF THE HOUR
LEVI'S HANGER WEBSITE

SUDDENLY, WE CAN TOTALLY IDENTIFY WITH
DR. FRANKENSTEIN'S RAPTURE. NO LONGER FROZEN ON PAPER,
DESIGN AND TYPOGRAPHY COME TO LIFE WITH SOUND, MOTION
AND INTERACTIVITY. "YIKES—IT'S ALIVE! IT'S ALIVE!"

**Salvador Dali and Madonna meet Fellini in an MTV nightmare.**

We had fun designing and directing this :20 "MTV Top of the Hour" spot. There's so much going on in the spot, that you must view it several times to see it all. But that's the point. This spot was meant to air repeatedly, and we didn't want anybody getting bored. The plan must have worked – it has been in heavy rotation for years. Produced by Colossal Pictures.

DOWNLOAD THE QUICKTIME MOVIE (2.3 MB)

**If Levi's 501 jeans are a straight-leg button-fly; What's a 505? A 550?**

We designed "The Hanger" portion of the Levi's website to provide comprehensive fit and style information on Levi's huge product offering. We made it very easy to peruse the entire range of fit and style options – from bell bottoms to straight 'n' narrow and everything in between – for men and women. Want to know which jean would look best on you? Take a look.

GO TO THE LEVI'S HANGER

**12 roaches can live on the glue of a postage stamp for a week.**

Bet you didn't know that. And maybe you'd rather not. But to a kid – it's pretty cool info. The Secret Language Action Club Kit (SLACK) combines great natural trivia with a secret code language & word puzzles. The Wild Art Club Kit (WACK) encourages kids to make photograms of dead bugs. We packaged these and other K4N products with kids' unique sensibilities in mind.

POSTER | STUFF | INTRO

The Designory/Pinkhaus http://www.designory.com / www.pinkhaus.com
Two firms on opposite coasts team up under one umbrella at this thought-provoking
site. Calling themselves "a community of creative people whose passion and
honesty combine to realize our full potential," the twin agencies have created
a website which invites audience participation and includes an ongoing,
threaded discussion group that allows visitors to address a variety of design
issues. Team Joel Fuller, Tim Meraz, Lannon Tanchum, Executive Creative
Directors; David Glaze, Creative Director; Chip McCarthy, Art Director; Jason
Deal, Producer; Rich Conklin, Frank Cunningham, Copywriters; Dalin Clark,
Account Executive; John Beck, Kevin Helms, Alan Rifkin, Copy Editors; David
Mealer, Sal Gonzales, Computer Production; Genex Interactive, Programming
and Hosting

Is Juvalamu that new Pepsi soft drink or is it

the jolly fat guy in Disney's new TV show?

Actually, it's neither. Yet. It's just a word that's

inherently silly and pleasing. And although

you've never seen the word before, you had an

immediate response to it, didn't you?

Psychologists recently discovered that the

moment we perceive something -- a person,

word, sound or picture -- we have an instanta-

neous positive or negative feeling about it. These

evaluations are unconscious, and apply even to

things we have never encountered before, like

nonsense words ("juvalamu" is considered highly

pleasing and "bargulum" moderately so, but

"chakaka" is generally disliked).

As open-minded as you may think you are, you

do not reserve judgement; in the first flash of

contact between an outside stimulus and your

mind you grade things as either positive or

negative -- you have no neutral perceptions.

How are you feeling about this?

Positive?

Negative?

Perfectly neutral?

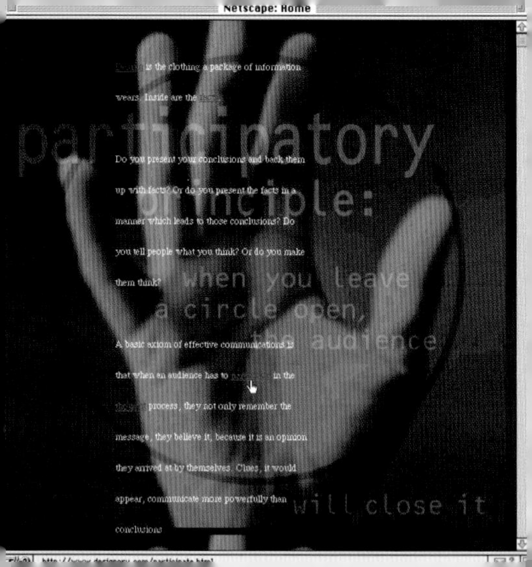

_____ is the clothing a package of information

wears. Inside are the _____

participatory

principle:

Do you present your conclusions and back them

up with facts? Or do you present the facts in a

manner which leads to those conclusions? Do

you tell people what you think? Or do you make

them think?

when you leave

a circle open,

an audience

A basic axiom of effective communications is

that when an audience has to _____ in the

_____ process, they not only remember the

message, they believe it, because it is an opinion

they arrived at by themselves. Clues, it would

appear, communicate more powerfully than

conclusions

will close it

All forms of media are migrating to the Web, from films and television to books and magazines; no big-budget movie or touring musical opens anymore without a website to promote it. Mainstream media have sensed the presence of an interloper, yet their response has been reluctant, when it isn't downright clumsy. Repurposing traditional media for the Web can range from the shovelware of magazines whose websites exist merely as marketing tools to sophisticated 'megasites' that harness multimedia technology to provide Web-specfic experiences. These Web immigrants are also finding out that many of the rules of 'old' media apply to the 'new' media; immediate, topical, relevant content still rules. Feed, Hotwired and Salon are online publicatons that are native to the Web, with no real-world counterparts. These 'digizines' are the Web's poster children. Mere infants compared to traditional media outlets, they're also most at risk: revenue streams are iffy and these startups don't have the deep pockets of the more established channels. Yet the genre has developed in record time into a full-blown phenomenon, critically acclaimed for its journalistic excellence and design smarts.

**Wired Digital** http://www.hotwired.com Wired Digital provides the umbrella for the online activities of Wired Ventures Inc., which include HotWired, the online daily that was the first commercial site on the Web; Wired News, a daily service; HotBot, a search engine; NewBot, an intelligent agent, and LiveWired, an ongoing experiment in 'push' technology. Team HotWired Barbara Kuhr and John Plunkett, Creative Directors; David Weir, Vice President of Programming; Sabine Messner, Senior Designer; Jeff Veen, Interface Designer; June Cohen, Executive Editor; Jill Atkinson, Producer; Dave Thau, Lead Engineer WiredNews Barbara Kuhr, Creative Director; David Weir, Vice President of programming; Erik Adigard, Design Director; Eric Eaton, Senior Designer; Chip Bayers, Martha Baer, Executive Editors; Kevin Kelleher, Senior Editor; Emily Tucker, Producer; Sean Welch, Lead Engineer HotBot/NewBot Barbara Kuhr, Creative Director; Ed Anuff, Product Manager; Erik Adigard, Design Director; Kevin Lyons, Designer; Mike Kuniavsky, Interface Designer; Inktomi, Engineering (HotBot); Todd Elliot, Production Manager (HotBot); Bowen Dwelle, Lead Engineer

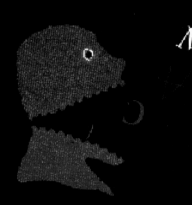

Atlas http://www.atlasmagazine.com Launched as a showcase for serious
photojournalism, this digizine has evolved into a quarterly publication that also
features new media art, animation, illustration and design, as well as
an eclectic mix of arts-related experimental works. **Studio** Atlas Web Design
**Team** Olivier Laude, Creative Director and Editor; Michael Macrone,
Webmaster and Technical Director; Amy Franceschini, Senior Designer;
Henrik Drescher, Illustrator (above)

MICHAEL_yamashita

GEORGE_steinmetz

atlas photography

valerie berta

adam kufeld **Appalachia**

by **Karen Kasmauski**

robin bowman

热爱祖国,热爱人民,拥护中国共产党,努力学习,准备为社会主义现代化贡献

坚持锻炼身体,积极参加有益的文娱活动。

Chinese Pop Posters

back ⊖ ⊕ forth

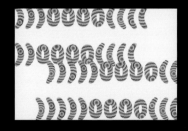

TerboTed

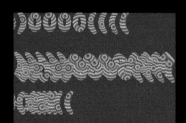
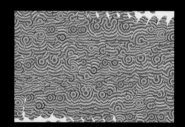

March 1997

April 1997

May 1997

December 1996

January 1997

February 1997

September 1996

October 1996

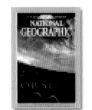

November 1996

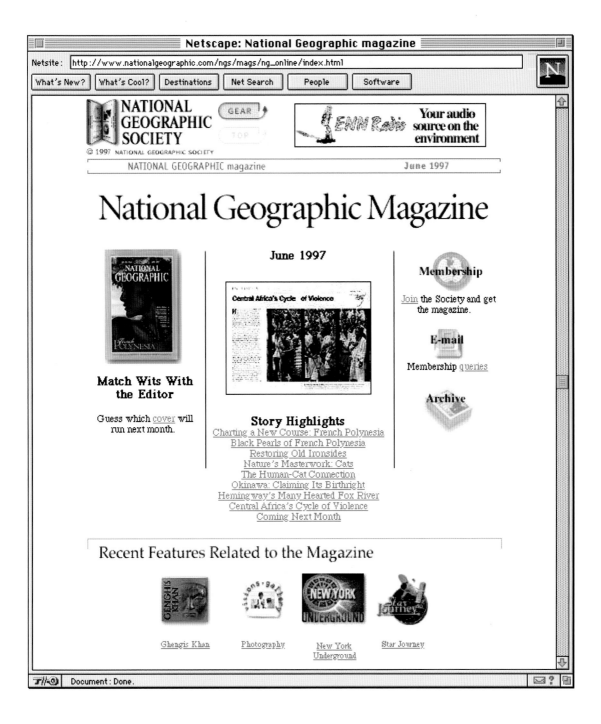

**National Geographic Online** http://www.nationalgeographic.com Developed by
the National Geographic Society as an electronic umbrella for the Society's
manifold media outlets – National Geographic, World and Traveler magazines,
television and cartographic divisions – this 'megasite' includes numerous
independently produced modules that vary considerably in style, content and
presentation.

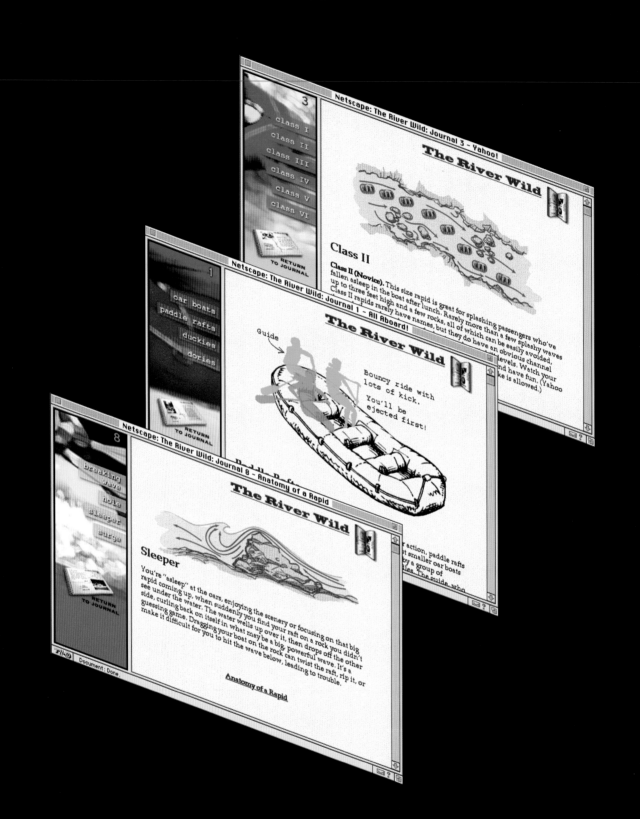

**The River Wild: Running the Selway** Called the wildest river in the lower 48 states, the Selway courses for 90 miles through the pine-robed mountains of central Idaho. This module for National Geographic Online follows Jeff Rennicke and Michael Melford's "virtual journal" down the river. It's an entertaining river-rafting resource for white-water enthusiasts and Web surfers alike. Studio Second Story Client National Geographic Society Team Brad Johnson and Eric Johnson, Designers; Chuck Carter, Illustrator; Kurt Strahm, Programmer; Jeff Rennicke, Photographer; Michael Melford, Writer

**Dinosaur Eggs** Visitors join an online egg hunt and share the excitement of fossil researchers as they 'hatch' fossilized dinosaur eggs to reveal the embryos inside. **Studio** Second Story **Client** National Geographic Society **Team** Brad Johnson and Julie Beeler, Designers; Julie Beeler, Programmer; Louie Psihoyos and Mark Thiesson, Photographers; Carolyn Anderson, Writer; Cathryn Buchanan, Producer

**The Fantastic Forest** National Geographic's first online module for kids allows users of all ages to explore the first virtual forest on the Internet. In search of hidden creatures and features, users navigate through fantastic 3-D environments co-created with artist Bud Peen. The site has QuickTime VR panoramas throughout, and a special Shockwave 'build your own forest' feature at the end. **Studio** Second Story **Client** National Geographic Society **Team** Brad Johnson and Julie Beeler, Designers; Brad Johnson and Bud Peen, Illustrators; Julie Beeler and Jellili Saleko, Programmers; Peter Winkler, Writer; Ford Cochran and Dorrit Green, Producers

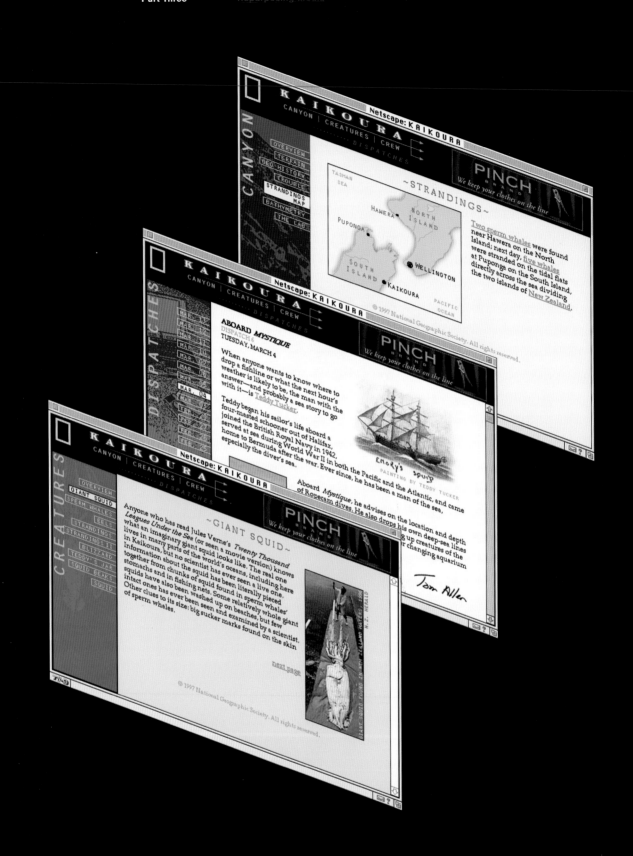

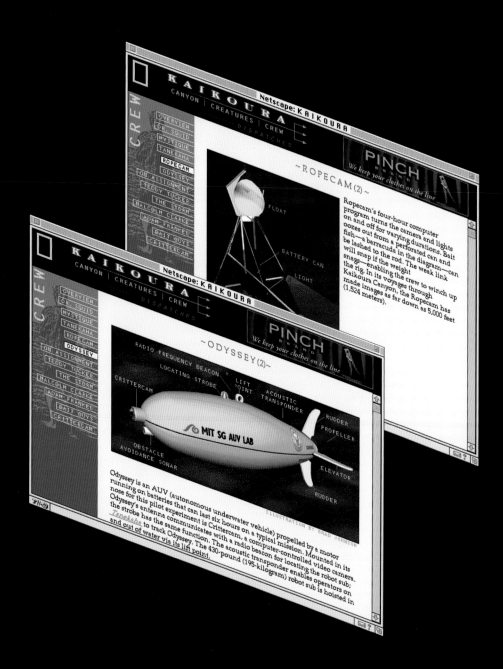

Kaikoura Expedition Off the shore of New Zealand lies a maze of mystery:
Kaikoura Canyon, a scarcely-explored system of deep-sea trenches. This module
for National Geographic Online followed a team of scientists on their
expedition in search of the giant squid. Designer Brad Johnson was 'on assign-
ment' in New Zealand for the magazine's first website created in the
field (or rather, at sea). **Studio** Second Story **Client** National Geographic Society
**Team** Brad Johnson and Julie Beeler, Designers; Julie Beeler, Programmer;
Brad Johnson and Emory Kristof, Photographers; Thomas B. Allen, Writer

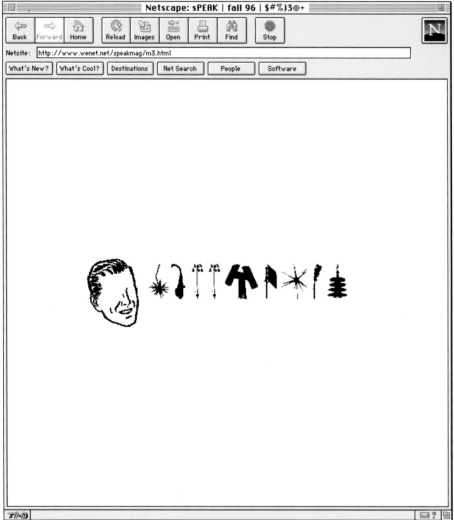

**Speak** http://www.speakmag.com Speak Magazine is published quarterly
and features articles, interviews and photo stories on art, fiction, music, film
and fashion. In addition to a table of contents and notices about articles in
upcoming issues, the website includes outtakes from the magazine – extra
photos, expanded articles, Web links, biographies of contributors. The site
is meant to suggest the look and feel of the magazine – more like a teaser in
support of, rather than a replacement for, the printed artifact. Team
Dan Rolleri, Publisher and Editor; Martin Venezky, Art Director, Illustrator;
Dave Granvold, Designer, Webmaster

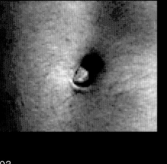

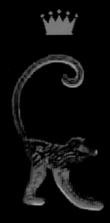

Disaster! By the time I was 30, I was an incredible drug addict.

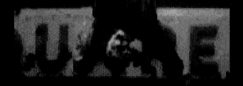

:tionmusicfashionfilmconversation

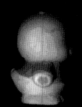

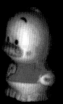

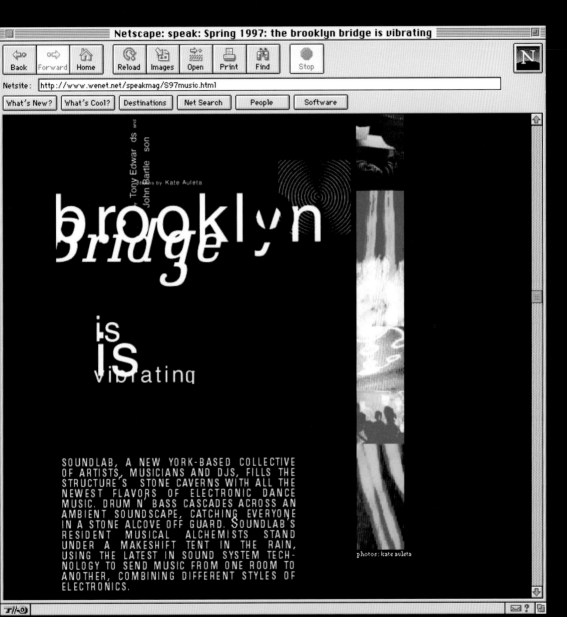

Netscape: speak: Spring 1997: the brooklyn bridge is vibrating

Netsite: http://www.wenet.net/speakmag/S97music.html

What's New?  What's Cool?  Destinations  Net Search  People  Software

by Tony Edwards
John Bartleson
photos by Kate Auleta

brooklyn
bridge

is
IS
vibrating

SOUNDLAB, A NEW YORK-BASED COLLECTIVE
OF ARTISTS, MUSICIANS AND DJS, FILLS THE
STRUCTURE'S STONE CAVERNS WITH ALL THE
NEWEST FLAVORS OF ELECTRONIC DANCE
MUSIC. DRUM N' BASS CASCADES ACROSS AN
AMBIENT SOUNDSCAPE, CATCHING EVERYONE
IN A STONE ALCOVE OFF GUARD. SOUNDLAB'S
RESIDENT MUSICAL ALCHEMISTS STAND
UNDER A MAKESHIFT TENT IN THE RAIN,
USING THE LATEST IN SOUND SYSTEM TECH-
NOLOGY TO SEND MUSIC FROM ONE ROOM TO
ANOTHER, COMBINING DIFFERENT STYLES OF
ELECTRONICS.

photos: kate auleta

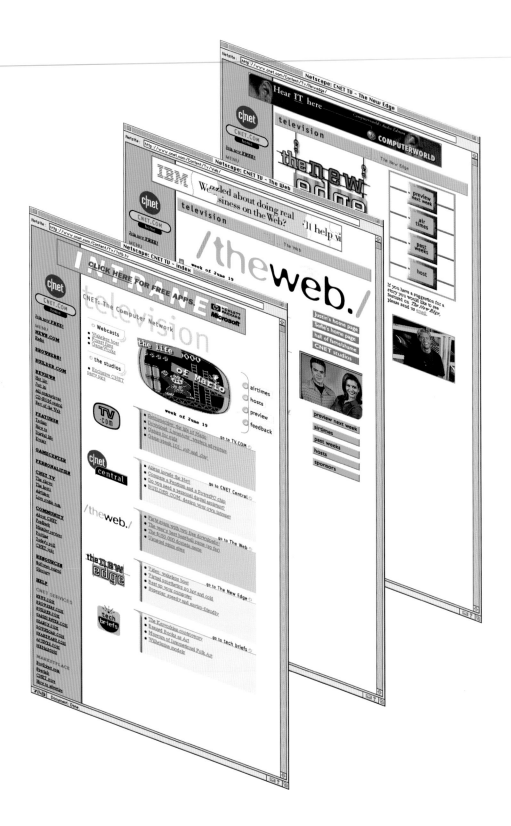

**CNET** http://www.cnet.com CNET: The Computer Network integrates television
programming with a network of ten sites on the World Wide Web: cnet.com
an online source for product reviews and information about computers and the
Internet; news.com a 24-hour technology news service; gamecenter.com
the Internet's gaming supersite; download.com a resource for free-download
software titles; shareware.com a searchable index of freeware and shareware titles; activex.com a source for researching, locating and downloading
ActiveX controls; browsers.com a one-stop shop for browser software;

buydirect.com a site where users can purchase and download the latest Internet software; search.com a categorized collection of over 400 Internet search engines and tools, and mediadome a joint site with Intel Corporation showcasing interactive experiences that meld content from media properties with new technology. **Studio** CNET: The Computer Network **Team** Fred Sotherland, Senior Vice-President, Creative Director; Cotton Coulson, Vice-President, Design Director; Chris Barr, Editor; Jonathan Rosenberg, Executive Vice-President, Technology; Jim Mingin, Director, Production, Creative Services

CAPTION: [Russian Federation, Moscow] A retired invalid stands in front of the Pension Fund in Moscow. On February 5th, the State Duma debated a resolution concerning the pensions of working retirees, which are being drawn upon by the government.

NEXT

CAPTION: [Russian Federation, Moscow] Russian pop star Alla Pugacheva holds a woman's shoe which she designed for her spring-autumn 1997 collection. Alla offers three different lines of women's shoes— Bon Chic, Les Femmes, and Hollywood. Prices range from 100 to 150 U.S. dollars per pair.

NEXT

CAPTION: [Russian Federation, Moscow] A placard reading "Half a year without pay. How do we live?!" was displayed in a windshield of an ambulance during a paramedics' strike in January. Paramedics, nurses, and their families blocked ambulance service in the city of Chita as a protest against a 6-month wage payment delay.

NEXT

CAPTION: [Russian Federation, Grozny] A family sold American cigarettes shortly before the inauguration of Chechen President Aslan Maskhadov on February 12th.

NEXT

NEXT

CAPTION: [Russian Federation, Pskov Region] Archimandrite Kenzorin, head of the Svyatogorskiy monastery, relaxes in his living quarters. The monastery is the burial place of Russian poet Aleksandr Pushkin.

NEXT

CAPTION: [Russian Federation, Moscow] Artist Tatyana Nazarenko presented her new plywood statues at an exhibition titled "My Paris," which opened on January 28th at Manege Hall. Oleg Shendykin, artistic director of the Roslan gallery, bums a smoke.

NEXT

CAPTION: [Russian Federation, Chechnya] A man wearing the photo of former Chechen leader Dzhokar Dudayev leaves a polling station during Chechen Presidential elections outside the village of Vedeno on January 27th. Dudayev was killed by Russian troops.

NEXT

CAPTION: [Russian Federation, Saransk] Nina Tarapkina (seated) was born without arms and learned to write by holding a pen with her teeth. Having earned a degree in philology from the University of Saransk, she is currently a teacher at the Potminsky boarding school for handicapped children.

NEXT

CAPTION: [Russian Federation, Moscow] "Gagarin before the Space Launch," painted by pilot-cosmonaut Vladimir Dzhanibekov, is part of an exhibition entitled "Sergei Korolev — Destiny and Time," held at Maly Manezh Hall. The exhibition is occasioned by the 90th birthday of Sergei Korolev, the founder of the Russian space program.

NEXT

CAPTION: [Russian Federation, Orenburg Region] A young resident of a village in the Novosergievsky District holds a loaf of bread baked with flour his parents receive as pay instead of money. Payments of this kind have become widespread across Russia as local authorities have no cash to pay farmers.

[All photos: copyright ITAR-TASS 1997.]

Check out election coverage, Big Bird, and O.J. in Flash 1.0.1

MOSCOW CHANNEL

CAPTION: [Russian Federation, Yaroslavl] Diesel-engine builders, attending a Jan 28th rally in the Central Russian city of Yaroslavl, demanded the resignation of the Russian government. Employees of local diesel-engine plants have not received wages for more than six months. One of the placards read: "Let those who destroyed the country be made to answer."

NEXT

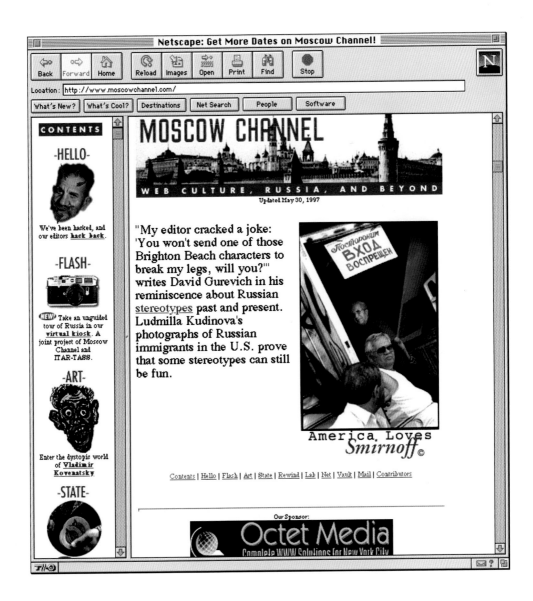

**Moscow Channel** http://www.moscowchannel.com Moscow Channel is
an online journal devoted to bringing Russian culture to the rest of the world. In
addition to original projects, the site features essays, fine art, photography,
interviews, and conjecture by world-renowned journalists, poets and artists. The
publication also administers an award program for outstanding Russia-
related websites Studio Moscow Media Team Alex Halberstadt, Editor, Creative
Director, Designer; Vladimir Druk, Editor

Location: http://www.fray.com/

 The 24 line mixes the

best and worst of San

Francisco. I'd forgotten

how unsettling it can be.

reality check

hope

Also in the fray:

Susan Paulsen is
**celebrating mom**

{fray} hope

Respect, yes;
equivalence,
no

Right On! By David Horowitz

HOROWITZ ARCHIVES

ABOUT DAVID HOROWITZ

SALON COLUMNISTS

SALON FRONT PAGE

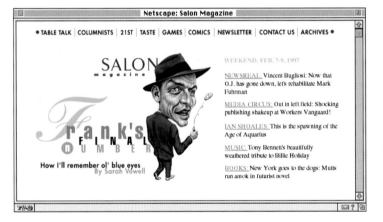

Netscape: Salon Magazine

● TABLE TALK | COLUMNISTS | 21ST | TASTE | GAMES | COMICS | NEWSLETTER | CONTACT US | ARCHIVES ●

SALON
magazine

Frank's FINAL NUMBER

How I'll remember ol' blue eyes
By Sarah Vowell

WEEKEND, FEB. 7-9, 1997

NEWSREAL: Vincent Bugliosi: Now that
O.J. has gone down, let's rehabilitate Mark
Fuhrman

MEDIA CIRCUS: Out in left field: Shocking
publishing shakeup at Workers Vanguard!

IAN SHOALES: This is the spawning of the
Age of Aquarius

MUSIC: Tony Bennett's beautifully
weathered tribute to Billie Holiday

BOOKS: New York goes to the dogs: Mutts
run amok in futurist novel

home
cooking
THE PLEASURES
AND PERILS OF FEEDING
OTHER PEOPLE

Illustration by Charlie Powell

**Salon** http://www.salonmagazine.com The critically acclaimed online literary magazine has evolved from a hybrid weekly-daily format to a full daily production schedule, and added new sections in the process. The publishers are betting that as the Web continues to grow, its denizens will be less obsessed with technology as an end in itself and more interested in using the medium to do what literate people have always enjoyed doing: reading and responding to great writing on attractive pages. **Studio** Salon Internet **Team** David Talbot, Editor/ CEO; Michael O'Donnell, Publisher/President; Andrew Ross, Managing Editor; Gary Kamiya, Executive Editor; Mignon Khargie, Design Director; Elizabeth Kairys, Art Director; Karen Templer: Associate Art Director; Steve Michel, Associate Webmaster

Flesh AND Ink

MOVIES

SENTIMENTAL TOURNEY

Spies
IN THE HOUSE OF LOVE

smashing
pumpkins

the
s

virginity

artist
search

track

pice
girls

e
nigma

enig

who's
on tour

lee
hooker

help
with this
site

e-mail
to
virgin

Virgin Records America http://www.virginrecord.com The challenge was to
extend a recognizable brand that is home to an incredibly diverse group
of individual artists and labels alike. Likewise, Virgin wanted to maintain their
image as a cutting edge company. Ikonic worked with Virgin to develop
a website that extends the Virgin brand in several ways, across music types,
artist idiosyncracies, and label identities. Studio Ikonic, Inc. Client Virgin
Records Team Tom Dolan, Co-Creative Director/Designer/Senior Art Director;
D. Thom Bissett, Lead  Designer; Al Wong, Michael Moroney, Producers;
Robin Raj, Co-Creative Director; Sara Ortloff, Design Director; Gretchen
Anderson, Production Management; Sharilyn Neidhardt, Interface
Designer; Doug Muise, Graphic Designer; Jon Thompson, Media Production;
Tim McCoy, Pam Miklaski, Sasha Panasik, Maureen Agius, HTML
production; Cameron Reid, Perl programming; Lars Nyman, ActiveX Developer

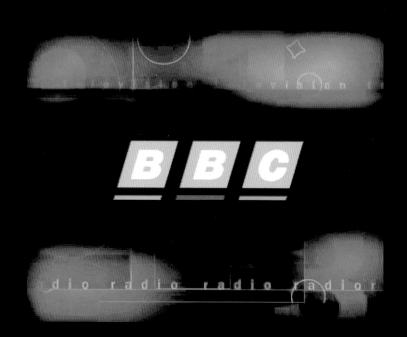

UK TELEVISION
UK RADIO
WORLD SERVICE
POLITICS
EDUCATION
ABOUT THE BBC
beeb @ the BBC
BBC WORLDWIDE

SCHEDULES
SEARCH
HIGHLIGHTS
JOB OPPORTUNITIES
RESEARCH AND DEVELOPMENT
TECHNICAL SERVICES
COPYRIGHT
CONTACT

BBC On-Line http://www.bbc.co.uk The site for Britain's national television network has several thousand pages, more than 75 programmes on-line, information about the regions, network radio, TV, world service radio, education, jobs, technical services, research and development and more. Studio BBC Internet Services Team Dr. Gordon Joly, Senior Producer; Simon Lockhart, Computer Systems Engineer; Brandon Butterworth, Research & Development; Christopher Garcia, Marketing Manager; Surjit Patel, Producer; Geekay Wong, Producer; Janine Powell, Assistant Producer; Lucy Gatward, Paul Lupson, Online Assistants, Designers; Dominik von Malaise, Webmaster and Director of BBC Internet Services

Welcome to the Web pages for the BBC's UK Radio stations

*'There are more things*
*in heaven and earth, Horatio,*
*than are dreamed of*
*in your philosophy'*

William Shakespeare

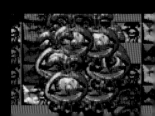

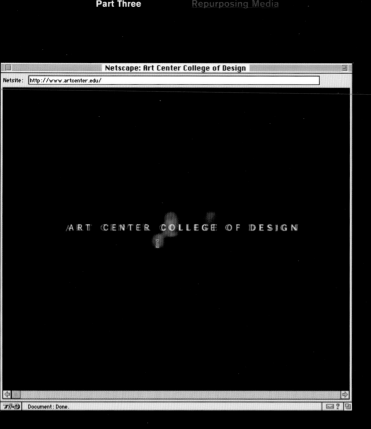

MAIN SCREEN
DEPARTMENTS
**GRAPHIC** AND
**PACKAGING DESIGN**

PROGRAM
PORTFOLIO
**CHAIR QUOTE**
CURRICULUM
FACULTY
STUDENTS
ALUMNI

*

"Whether we use traditional methods or digital **technology,**
without strong ideas, a design is mere decoration. We must always ask of ou
designs: '**What does this** say;
what does it **communicate?**
**Does it just look good, or does it convey an idea with**
**impact and clarity?**"Education must precede design. Before
they become designers, I ask my students to be explorers, to
nourish their imaginations by reading, investigating other
disciplines and cultures, and observing human nature. The
educated designer will always ask 'what if?' **and ta**ke time
to study many possible solutions to a pro**blem even be**fore
committing ideas to paper or hard di**sk.**"

James Miho, Chair, Graphic and Packaging Design Department

**GRAPHIC** AND
**PACKAGING DESIGN**

Art Center College of Design http://www.artcenter.edu/ At this stage
essentially an online recruitment catalog, the site currently provides general information about the college, its departments, and admissions requirements,
along with an 'E-ply' request form for prospective students. Displays of curriculum
and course descriptions, faculty biographies and images of student work
may also be viewed, and there are also links to student sites and online classes.

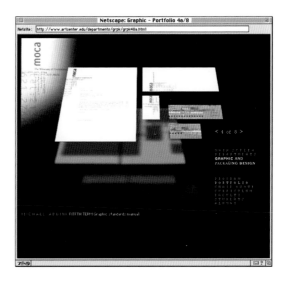

MAIN SCREEN
DEPARTMENTS
FINE ART

PROGRAM
PORTFOLIO
**CHAIR QUOTE**
CURRICULUM
FACULTY
STUDENTS
ALUMNI

n a time of accelerated change, ambiguous values, and visual excess, art provokes meaning out of the complexity of contemporary experience. Success in fine art requires a cultivation of the mind and an ability to

**trust** one's instincts. Art Center offers the serious student of fine art a stimulating community of thinkers and artists with whom to explore both the how and the why of art. The curriculum, which combines a rigorous studio program with

## critical inquiry

into what it means to pursue art, helps aspiring artists develop uncommon technical skills and a sound theoretical basis on which they can build a body of work."

Laurence Dreiband, Chair, Fine Art Department

FINE ART

Client Art Center College of Design Studio Art Center Design Office
Team Stuart I. Frolick, vice President, Creative Director; Darin Beaman, Art Director; Gudrun Frommherz, Technical Director; Darin Beaman and Gudrun Frommherz, Design and Web Design; Tiago Soromenho-Ramos, Associate Designer; Gudrun Frommherz, Programmer; Steven A. Heller, Photographer

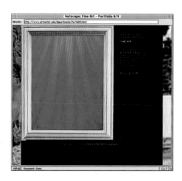

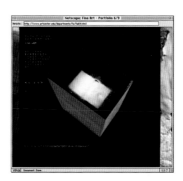

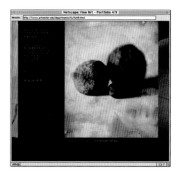

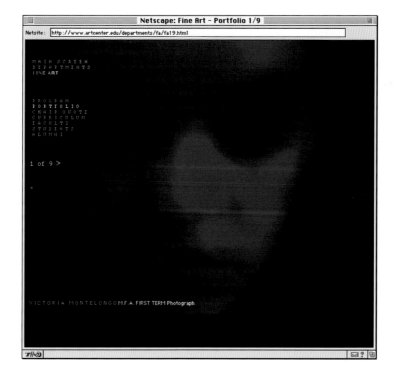

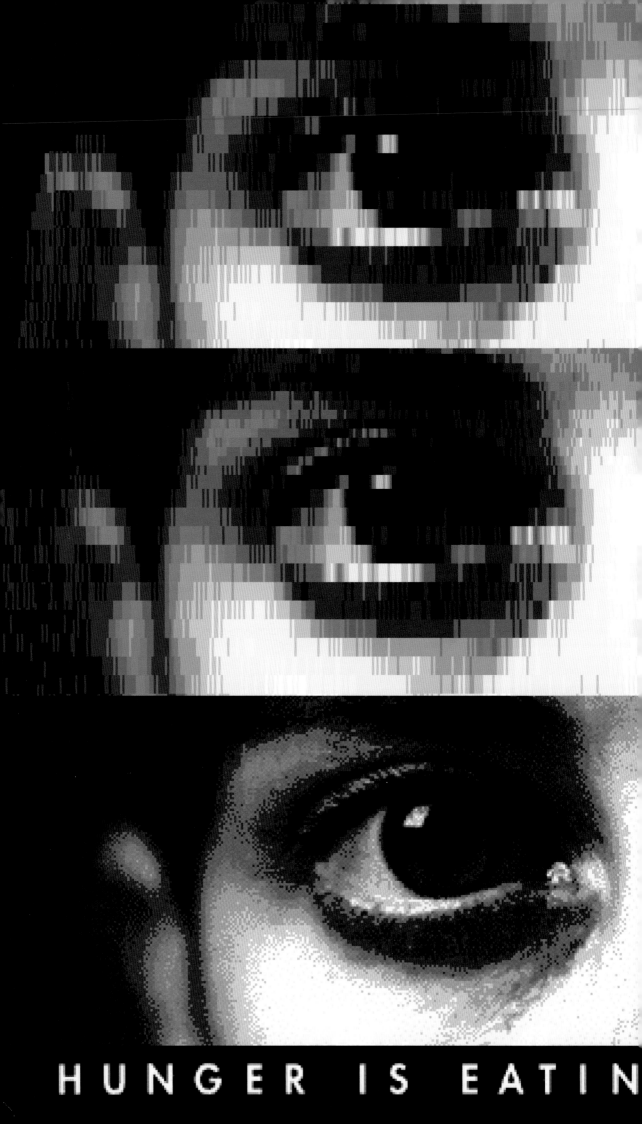

HUNGER IS EATIN

G AMERICA ALI

**Netscape: Second Harvest Disaster Relief Food and Supplies Shipments**

Location: `http://www.secondharvest.org/websecha/e_ship.htm`

SECOND HARVEST

**ISSUES AND EVENTS**

SECOND HARVEST
UPDATE MAGAZINE

EVENTS CALENDAR

**DISASTER RELIEF
UPDATES**

## Food and Supplies Shipments

A frequently updated list of food and supplies sent to flood victims in Minnesota, North Dakota and South Dakota via the Second Harvest national food bank network.

**Total poundage shipped as of 5/15/97**
1,715,042 (excluding rolling donation of 4 million pounds from Pillsbury)

**Food banks storing shipments**
Fargo, ND
Crookston, MN (near Grand Forks)
Sioux Falls, SD

**Donors/product**

- Borden Foods Corp./pasta
- Cargill, Inc./peanut butter
- Central Missouri Food Bank/paper cups, paper towels
- Church & Dwight/toothpaste
- DowBrands/laundry detergent, cleaning products
- EMCO Food Service/assorted foods
- Food Bank of North Carolina/assorted canned goods
- Food Bank of Oakland County/assorted foods
- General Mills/cereal
- Great Brands of Europe/bottled water
- Harvesters (Kansas City food bank)/assorted foods, groceries
- Heinz USA/soup, spaghetti sauce
- I.C. Refreshments/beverages
- S.C. Johnson/cleaning products, boots
- Kellogg/cereal, snacks
- Kraft/pasta salad
- M&M/Mars/candy, snacks
- Nabisco/snacks, hot cereal
- Nebraska Food Bank Network/mouthwash, canned foods
- Pillsbury/canned vegetables, baked beans
- Powerfood/nutrition bars
- Procter & Gamble/cleaning supplies, toilet tissue, facial tissue, oral hygiene kits, diapers
- Quaker Oats Company/beverages
- Riviana Foods/rice
- Second Harvest Food Bank of Lehigh Valley/cereal
- Second Harvest Food Bank of Milwaukee/beverages
- Southwest Beer Distributors/juice, water
- Tree Top/apple juice, applesauce
- Tri-State Food Bank/assorted canned goods
- White Castle/chicken sandwiches

**Corporations**
Flood victims need your donations of cleaning supplies, diapers, and food items in cans or single-serving sizes.
Call 1-800-771-2303, ext. 131 to donate. Thank you.

**Second Harvest** http://www.secondharvest.org Second Harvest, the largest domestic hunger relief organization in the United States, bills itself as 'hunger's hope.' The organization solicits donated food and grocery products from the food industry and distributes the products through a nationwide network of nearly 200 food banks reaching over 50,000 charitable feeding programs. In 1996, this network served more than 26 million men, women and children. Since the launch of the site, Second Harvest has increased individual and industry donations, improved communications to and from member food banks, and increased the awareness of hunger as a social — and political — issue. **Studio** Waters Design Associates **Client** Second Harvest **Team** Rick Whelan, Design Manager; Michelle Novak, Designer; Dominic Poon, Armando Jimarez, Levana Cheng, Programmers; Tom Lindfors, Photography; Mary Flockempa, Illustrator. Second Harvest: Adrianne T. Hayward, Director of Communications; Randall Crane, Noel Franus, Writers & Editors; John Muller, Manager of Information Systems

<u>The big bucks</u> that beckon on the Web may have eluded most companies so far, though a small but growing number of businesses are figuring out how to turn the medium's push-button interactivity into hard cash. Meanwhile, most corporate websites seem content to merely advertise their inventories, while a few approach the market with a soft sell, focussing on the company's history and prestige. For the unlucky corporation faced with a product recall or other public relations disaster, the Web can be an effective communication tool. <u>Web design</u> for The Corporate Sector begs a question: can a brand really be a destination? Can promotional content replace the real thing, or is the corporate website just another sales brochure? And what about advertising, seen by many as the bane of Web communications?

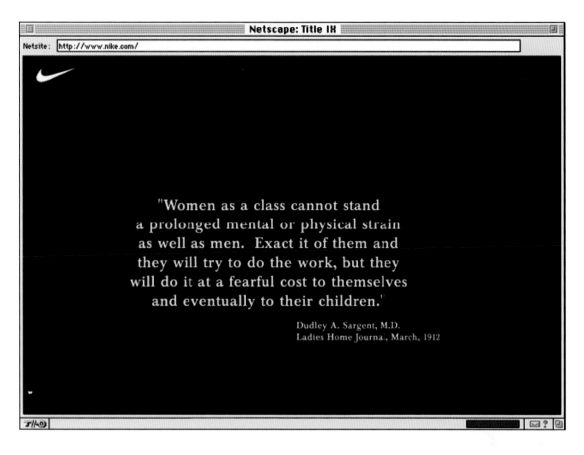

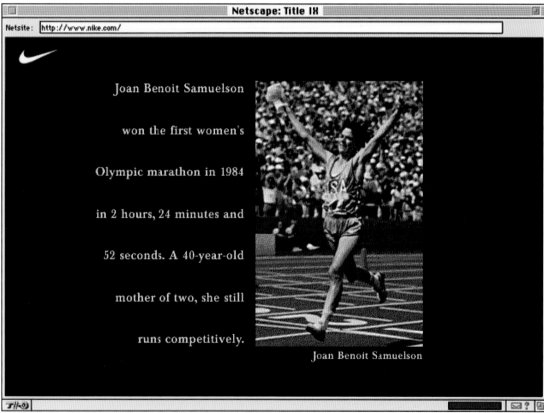

**Nike** http://www.nike.com This splash to the nike site was launched on June 23, the 25th anniversary of the signing of Title IX. **Studio** Nike **Team** Creative Director, Mary Duffy; Consultant Webmaster, Kristin Boden-MacKay, Nike; Designer, Joan Olbrantz, Nike; Editor, Barry Locke, Nike; Production Artist, Anita Barraco-Cator, Step Technology; Production Assistant, Alicia Smith, Nike

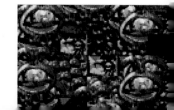

Then they said we shouldn't play...

Netsite: http://www.nike.com/

"There's nothing feminine or enchanting
about a girl with beads of perspiration
on her alabaster brow, the result of
grotesque contortions in events totally
unsuited to female architecture."

Sportswriter Arthur Daley
New York Times, February, 1953

---

Netscape: Title IX

Netsite: http://www.nike.com/

Lisa Leslie owns the
Pacific-10 Conference
career record for scoring
(2,414), rebounds (1,214),
and blocks (321),
and also holds USC records
for most blocks in a season
(95) and a career (321).
She is the only player in
Pac-10 history to receive
all-conference first-team
honors four times.

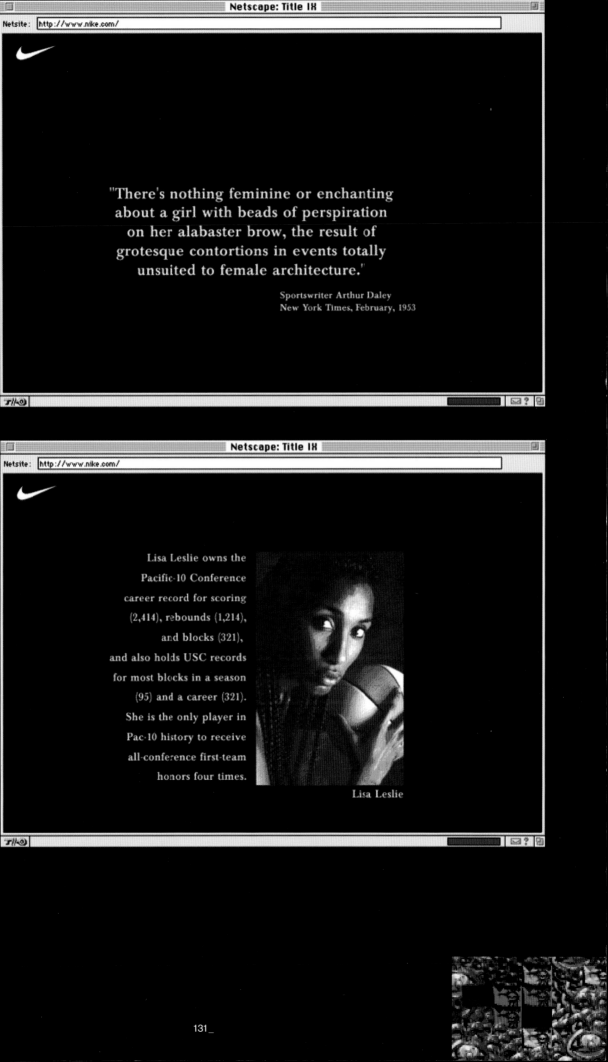

Lisa Leslie

Next they said we could play,
just not too hard...

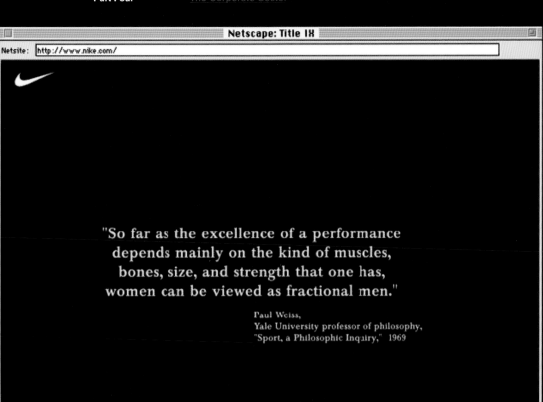

"So far as the excellence of a performance
depends mainly on the kind of muscles,
bones, size, and strength that one has,
women can be viewed as fractional men."

Paul Weiss,
Yale University professor of philosophy,
"Sport, a Philosophic Inquiry," 1969

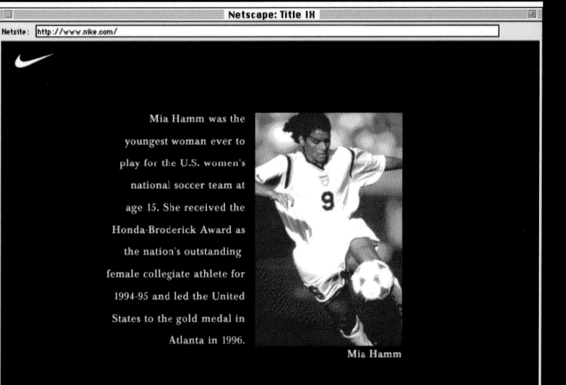

Mia Hamm was the
youngest woman ever to
play for the U.S. women's
national soccer team at
age 15. She received the
Honda-Broderick Award as
the nation's outstanding
female collegiate athlete for
1994-95 and led the United
States to the gold medal in
Atlanta in 1996.

Mia Hamm

Netsite: http://www.nike.com/

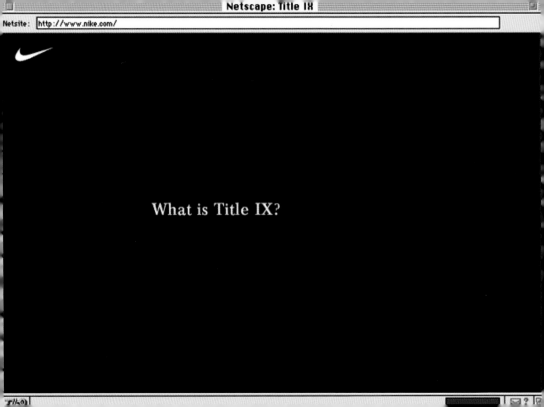

s part of the Education Amendments of 1972 and it states.

Io person in the United States shall, on the basis of sex,
e excluded from participation in, be denied the benefits of,
r be subjected to discrimination under any education program
r activity receiving Federal financial assistance. June 23, 1972

OK, but what does that mean?

t means -- among other things -- that schools
ave to give girls and women equal opportunities
o play sports. So, athletic budgets -- including
cholarship money -- have to be fairly divided
etween men's and women's programs.

# OUR SKATES
WE MAKE THE BEST SKATES. FOR YOU.

# PROTECTIVE GEAR
IF YOU SKATE, YOU'VE GOT TO GET THE GEAR.

# SKATEFINDER
INDIVIDUALIZED SKATE SUGGESTIONS.

# DEALER FINDER
THERE'S A DEALER IN YOUR NEIGHBORHOOD.

# TECH
THE INNOVATIONS BEHIND OUR SKATES.

Netscape: Rollerblade: Skate Scenes: Aggressive

Location: http://www.rollerblade.com/skate/aggressive/aggressive.html

# AGGRESSIVE
MARKED BY DRIVING FORCEFUL ENERGY

RIDERS
SKATES & GEAR
BACKSTAGE AT ULTIMATE
SKATE PARKS
EVENTS
CHAT
BULLETIN BOARD

site menu    skate scenes

Rollerblade http://www.rollerblade.com A site about a company like Rollerblade should be visually striking and action-packed, so think of this one as a collection not of Web pages, but of Web posters. The studio strove in the design to capture a tangible feeling of space and movement, focusing on the sport as much as the client's products. Yet even the product pages are bold, attractive and full of depth. Studio Adjacency: Brand New Media™ Client Rollerblade Team Andrew Sather, Creative Director and Designer; Bernie DeChant, Art Director and Designer; Matia Wagabaza, Designer; Pascal, Designer; Carlo Calica, Webmaster; Matt Kirchstein, Programmer

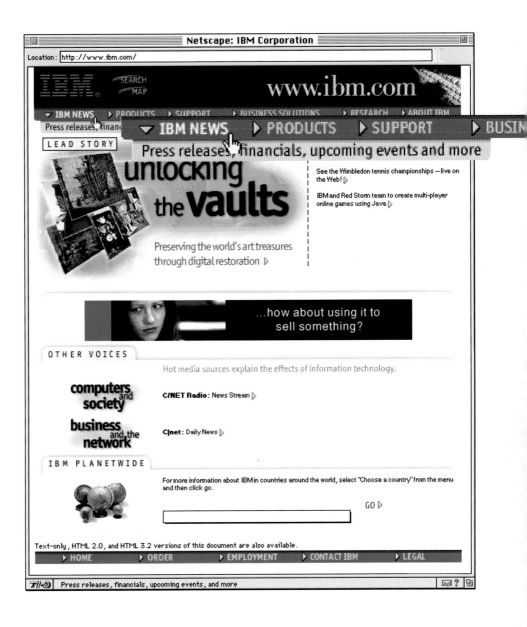

**IBM** http://www.ibm.com IBM's website serves as a gateway to one of the largest commercial sites on the web. IBM has over 140,000 pages online, covering the full range of product and service offerings, from personal computers to massively parallel supercomputers and highly specialized offerings like export consulting and original equipment manufacturing, as well as corporate information and company news releases and announcements Studio IBM Corporate Internet Programs/Studio Archetype Team IBM: Carol Moore, Director; Alex Wright, Manager, Creative Team; Ed Costello, Senior Webmaster; Eileen Mullin, Editor. Studio Archetype: Judith Hoogenboom, Creative Integrator; John Grotting, Creative Director

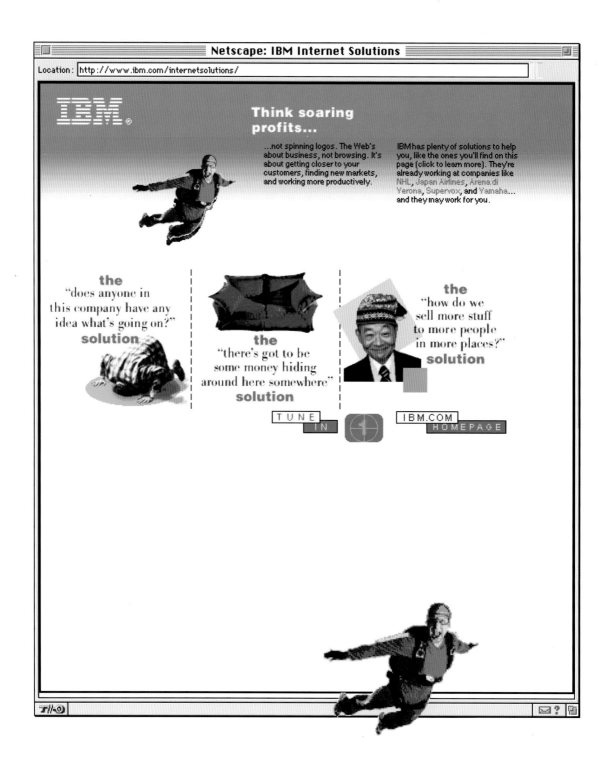

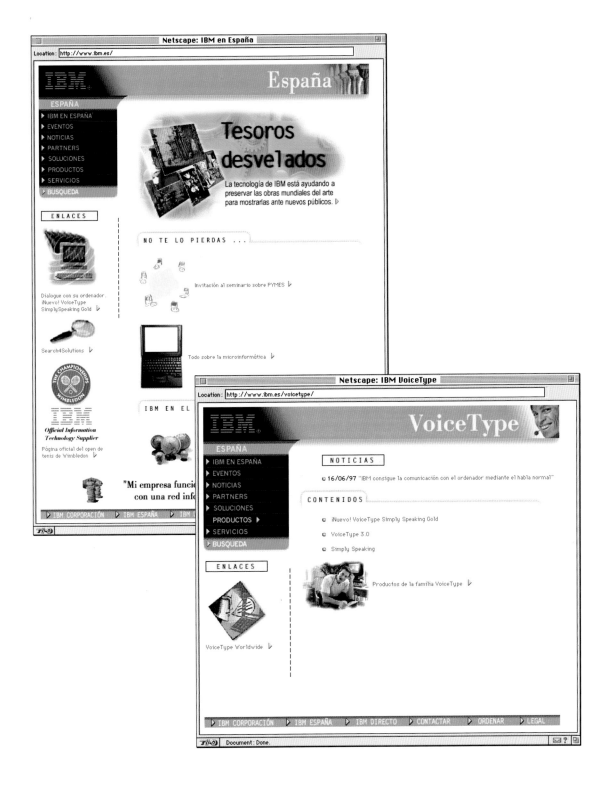

PORSCHE

index

Heritage

Ferdinand
Porsche

People

Craftsman

Reinhold Berleff

Drivers

Hurley
Haywood

David
Murry

Jeff
Zwart

Design
Philosophy

Driver
to Car

Car
to Road

Creating

Milestones

Early
Years

The
'60s

The
'70s/'80s

The
'90s

LeMans 97

LeMans
Heritage

The Circuit

LeMans
Entries

Race
Coverage

Boxster

Arizona

The car

Gallery

Postcards

Driving

Home

Model
Lineup

Carrera

Targa

Carrera 4

Carrera 4S

Turbo

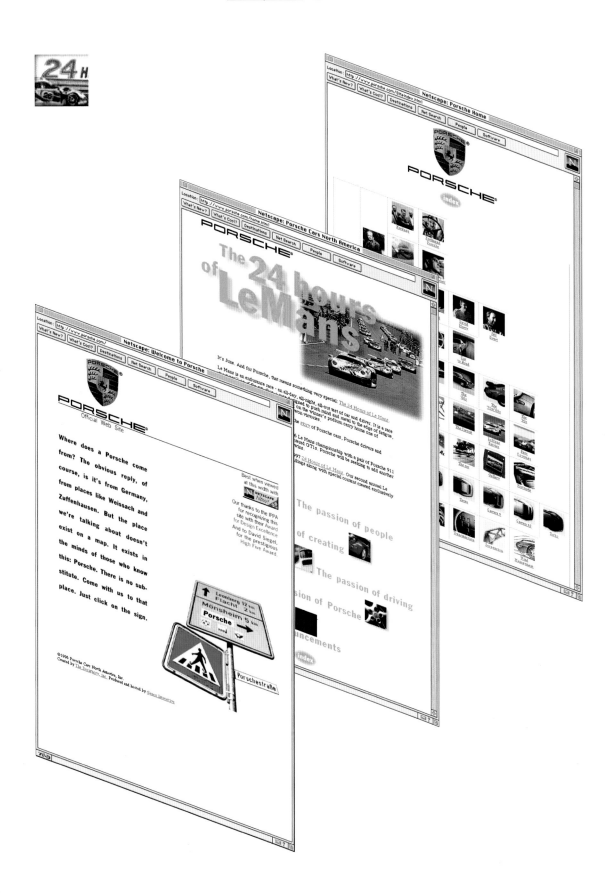

**Porsche** http://www.porsche.com The primary goal of the site is to expose a broad Web audience to the unique culture and mystique of the brand (not just potential buyers, which is a relatively small group). Porsche's heritage, its people, their philosophies and their passion for building the best sports cars in the world are the major themes.

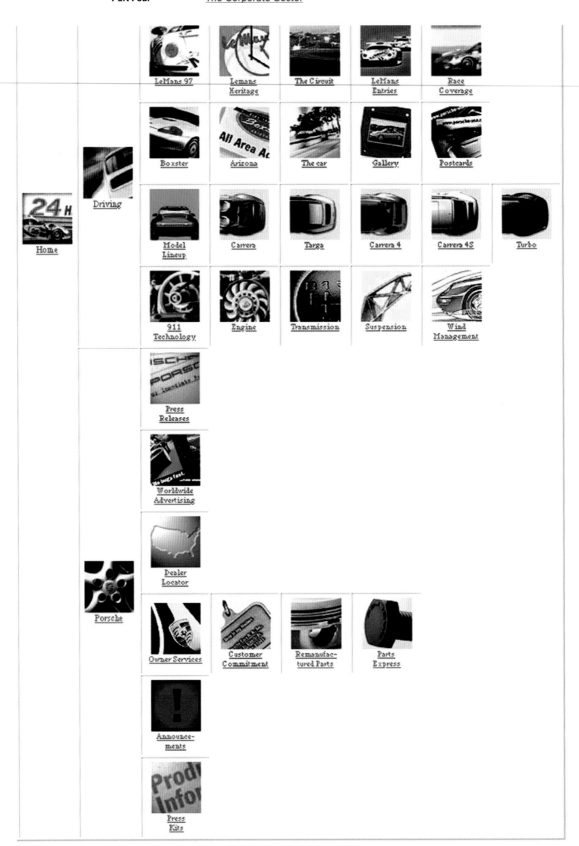

**Studio** The Designory, Inc. **Client** Porsche Cars North America **Team** Lannon Tanchum, Executive Creative Director; David Glaze, Creative Director; Chip McCarthy, Art Director; Rich Conklin, Copywriter; Peggy McCabe, Account Executive; Alan Rifkin, Proofreader; Genex Interactive, Programming and Hosting. Consulting: Wes Haynes, Creative Director; Steve Davis, Art Director; Tina Viramontes, Project Coordinator; Lisa Dimitrov, Computer Production; Jason Deal, Producer; Chad Weiss, Copywriter; Brian Kennedy, Product Specialist

Butler, Shine & Stern

1 2 3 4 5 6 7 8

SPYKE BEER

Work

Anheuser-Busch    Specialized
Miller's Outpost  Round Table
◀ click for full ad  Northgate Mall

1  2

next

work    who we are : staff : partners : dogs

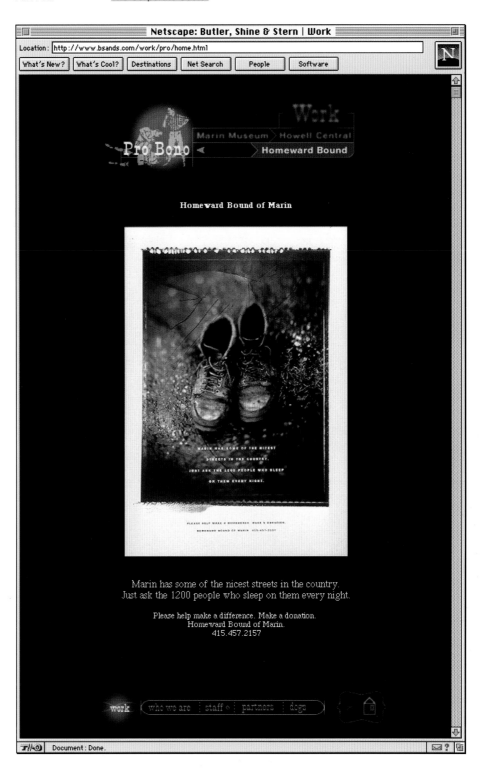

Butler, Shine & Stern http://www.bsands.com The site conveys the agency's personality by including a range of materials, such as samples of work, photos of the staff, bios of the partners, a statement of philosophy, and a page dedicated to the agency dogs. The Work section includes downloadable videos of TV commercials, radio spots, and thumbnails and large versions of a number of print ads and posters. **Studio** Atlas Web Design **Client** Butler, Shine & Stern, Inc. **Team** Olivier Laude, Creative Director; Michael Macrone, Webmaster and Technical Director; Amy Franceschini, Senior Designer

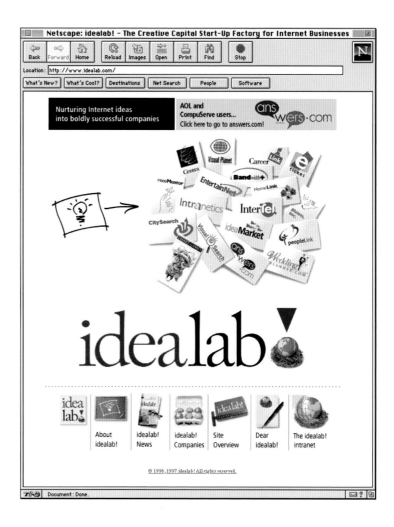

**idealab!** http://www.idealab.com The site is intended to be the most thorough informational resource on idealab! and all its foster companies. The website reflects the basic mission of the parent company in several ways. The focus of the site is an appealing 'card nest' which draws attention to the many company offspring hatched from the creativity of the idealab! family. This card nest showcases the design talents of the creative force which jumpstarts the dependent companies. The site includes updates and sample artwork for idealab! companies under construction. Team Tom Hughes, Doug Tally, Bill Gross, Dave Urban, Designers Douglas Tally, Webmaster; Bill Gross, Director

Welcome to ideaMarket!

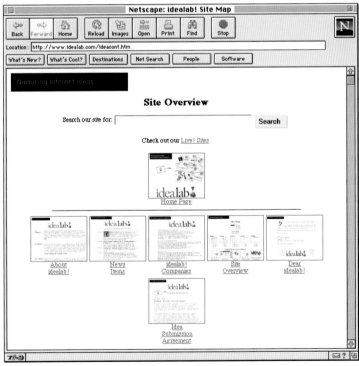

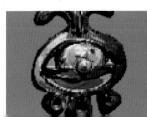

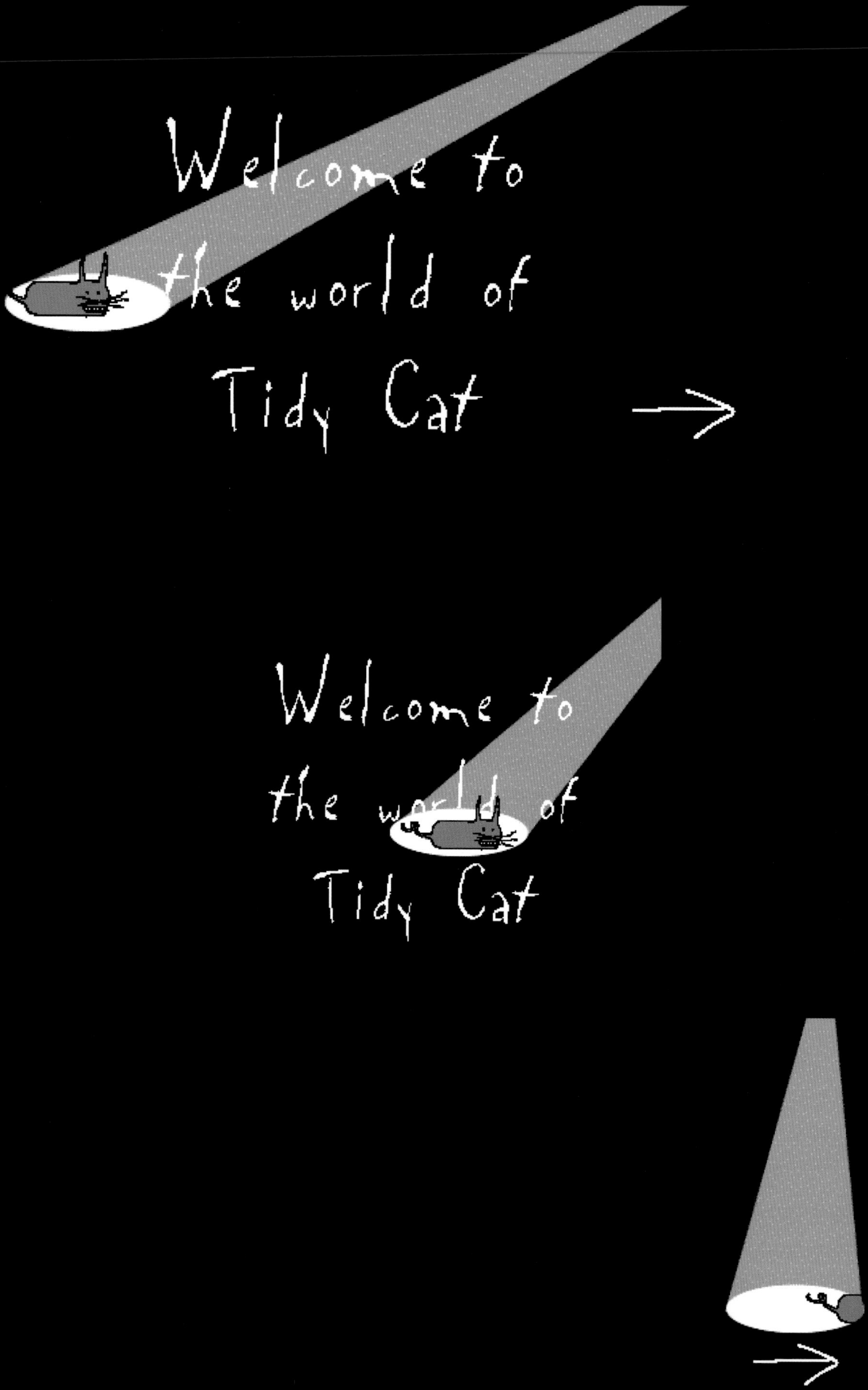

Welcome to
the world of
Tidy Cat →

Welcome to
the world of
Tidy Cat

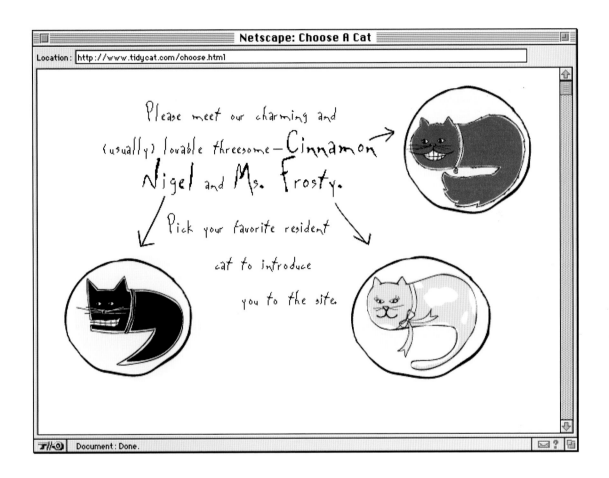

**Tidy Cat** http://www.tidycat.com Mundane problems never stop original minds.
This site exudes freshness and humor. Client Ralston Purina Studio Duffy
Design Team Joe Duffy, Art Director; Lourdez Banez, Designer; Chuck Carlson,
Deborah Gold, Copywriters

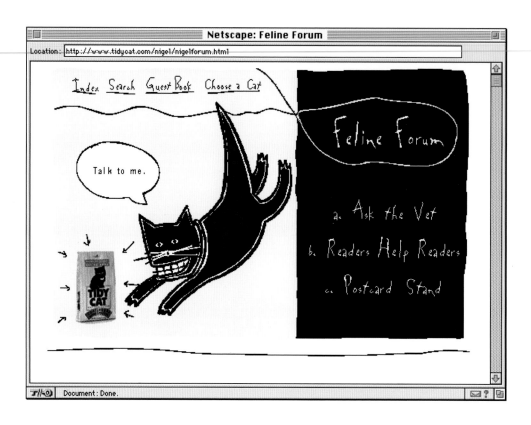

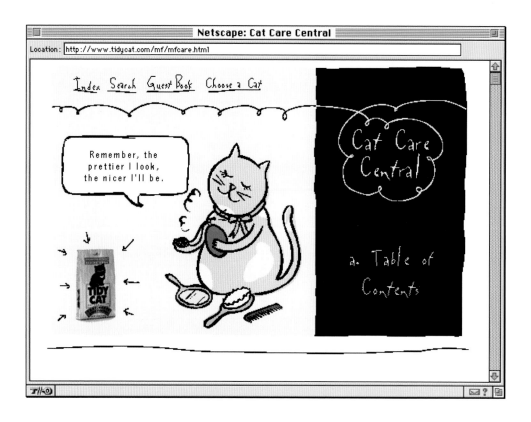

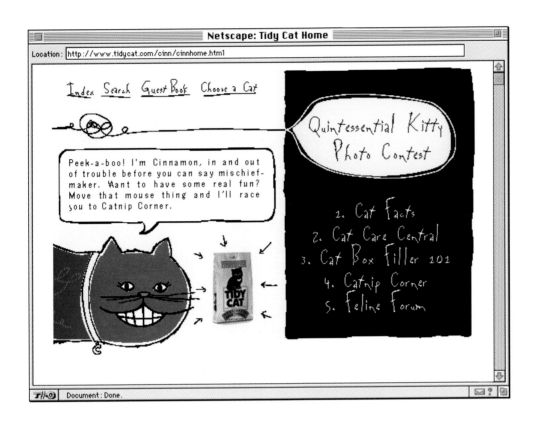

Welcome to
# SOTHEBY'S

Information  News
Frequently Asked Questions
Departments and Experts
Ordering Books, Catalogues
    & Magazines
Sotheby's International Realty

Auction Adventures

Featured Sales:
The Art of Disney's
*James and the Giant Peach*
and *The Hunchback
of Notre Dame*

Impressionist and
Modern Art, Part 1

Contemporary Art, Part 1

Highlighted Auctions
Worldwide Calendar
Gallery of Past Auctions
Auction Results

Auctions  538

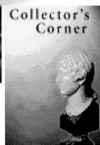

Collector's
Corner

For the Connoisseur
Featured Appraisal: A True Story
Emerging Collector
    Notes for the Beginning Collector
    Caring for Your Collection
    How to Assess Value
Internet Resources
Educational Programs

**Sotheby's** http://www.sothebys.com The website features links to an in-depth
database of auction items sold and for sale, along with a comprehensive
calendar of events, a how-to section for collectors, featured auctions and a Web
game. Studio i/o 360 digital design, inc. Client Sotheby's Team Dindo
Magallanes, Creative Director; Nathalie delaGorce, Designer; Shana Fisher,
Design Technologist

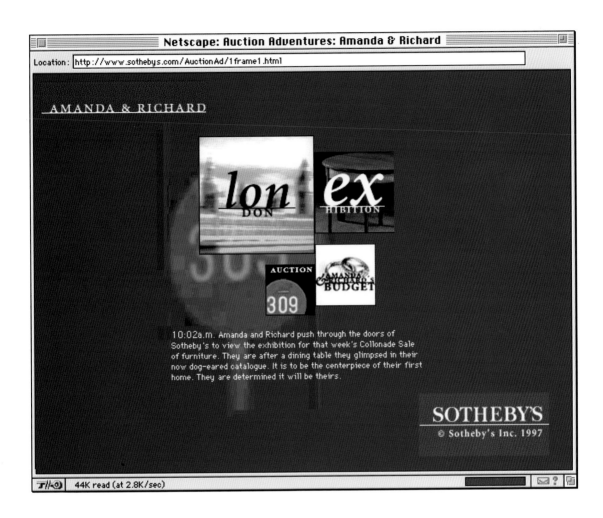

Netscape: Auction Adventures: Amanda & Richard

Location: http://www.sothebys.com/AuctionAd/1frame1.html

AMANDA & RICHARD

10:02a.m. Amanda and Richard push through the doors of
Sotheby's to view the exhibition for that week's Collonade Sale
of furniture. They are after a dining table they glimpsed in their
now dog-eared catalogue. It is to be the centerpiece of their first
home. They are determined it will be theirs.

SOTHEBY'S
© Sotheby's Inc. 1997

44K read (at 2.8K/sec)

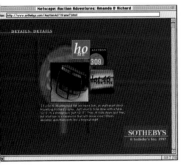

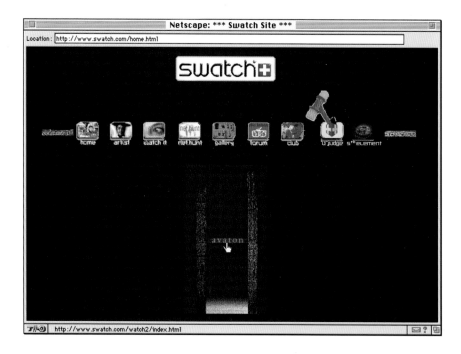

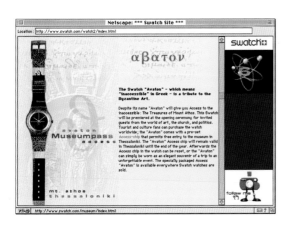

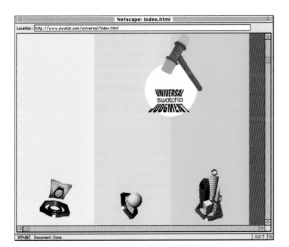

**Swatch** http://www.swatch.com The Swatch website is the official homepage of Swatch International. Along with company and product information, there are special events like an Internet hunt and discussion forums that have created a large Swatch online community around the world. Studio I-D Gruppe Client Swatch Team Bernd Kolb, Creative Director; Barbara Bolsinger, Project Manager; Bernd Riesterer, Webmaster; Yannick Hervy, Designer; Andrea Schrade, Editor

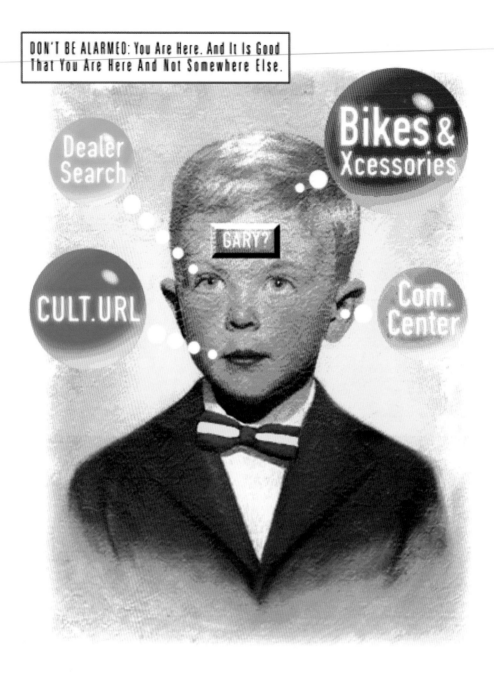

DON'T BE ALARMED: You Are Here. And It Is Good That You Are Here And Not Somewhere Else.

Dealer Search

Bikes & Xcessories

GARY?

CULT.URL

Com. Center

**Fisher Bicycle** http://www.fisherbikes.com The site presents an overview of the Fisher offering and culture, and includes information on Fisher mountain bicycles and accessories, updates on the activities of the Fisher Racing Team, bulletin boards and Q&A sections for mountain bike aficionados. Studio Thirst Client Fisher Bicycle Team Dean Gore, Executive Producer and Editor; Rick Valicenti, Director and Co-Producer; Chester, Co-Producer, Editors and Designer; Wm Valicenti, Photography; Tara Cottrell at Cedro Group, Webmaster

## Netscape: TRUISM 7

Location: http://www.adaweb.com/project/holzer/cgi/pcb.cgi

What's New?   What's Cool?   Destinations   Net Search   People   Software

ALL THINGS ARE DELICATELY INTERCONNECTED

PLEASE CHANGE BELIEFS

[ˈädaˈweb]

If Magritte's concept was that what we see (the pipe) is not what we see, and Warhol's evolution of that concept was that what we see (a star, a soup can) is short-lived, then the concept that what we see is 'optional' (either/or) is perhaps the domain of late 20th century culture – and the Web. This part of the book focuses on the work of individuals who are using the medium to express broader cultural concepts, to expand our visual and verbal vocabularies. Deconstructivism has galvanized more than a generation of thinkers. And the Web is one place where they meet. That Jenny Holzer's work should translate so elegantly to the Web becomes, in this context, an (un)necessary proof of the artists Post-Modern ethic. And discussion about whether Art can or cannot be created for the Web, answers itself. The 'symmetry' described by much of this work is closer to Eastern than Ancient Roman philosophy – energy, anarchy and chance, the structure. There is continuity. It is wonder. Robert Appleton

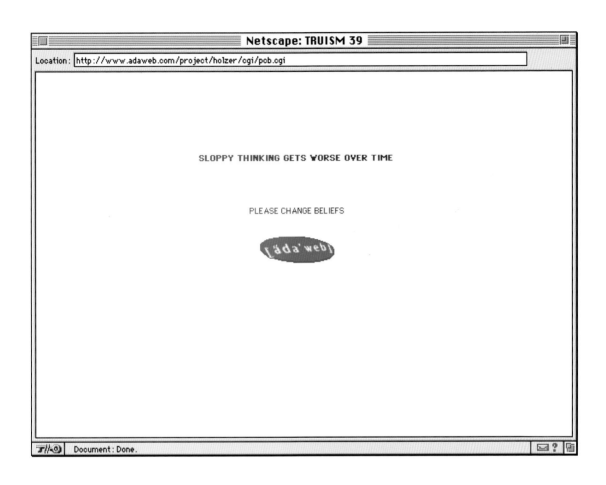

äda'web http://www.adaweb.com A critically acclaimed online gallery of work for the Web, the site is composed of six areas: Project presents works created specifically for the site; Influx houses works that exist in relation to real space events; Context is the site's fulcrum between work and dialogue, including associated projects, events, and information on artists; Exchange is an online store with an eclectic array of merchandise by and about artists; Nota is a forum for visitors to express their thoughts about the site; Extension is a specialized directory of links elsewhere on the Web. Studio Digital City Studio Team Benjamin Weil, Curator and Executive Producer; Vivian Selbo, Ainatte Inbal, Cherise Fong, Design/Production; Andrea Scott, Director of Business Development; Matteo Ames, Webmaster; John Simon Jr., Technical Consultant; Cheryl Kaplan, Public Relations

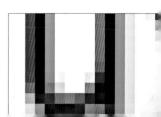

BOREDOM MAKES YOU DO CRAZY THINGS

SLIPPING INTO MADNESS IS GOOD FOR THE SAKE OF COMPARISON

YOU ARE A VICTIM OF THE RULES YOU LIVE BY

LACK OF CHARISMA CAN BE FATAL

ACTION CAUSES MORE TROUBLE THAN THOUGHT

see ( 400 K )

PLEASE CHANGE BELIEFS

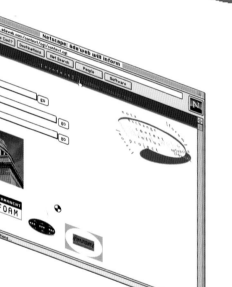

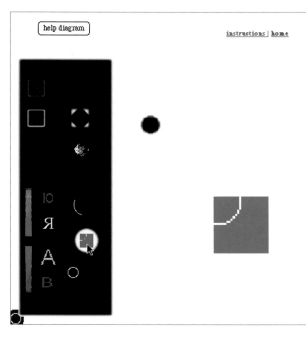

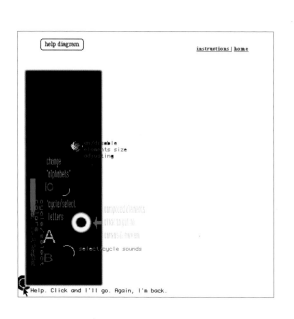

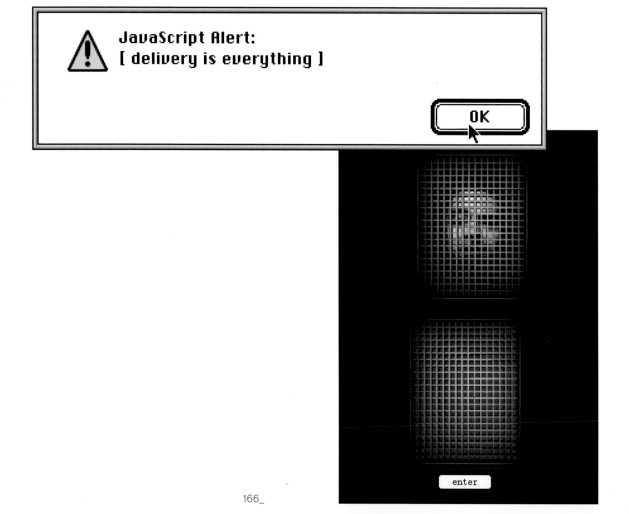

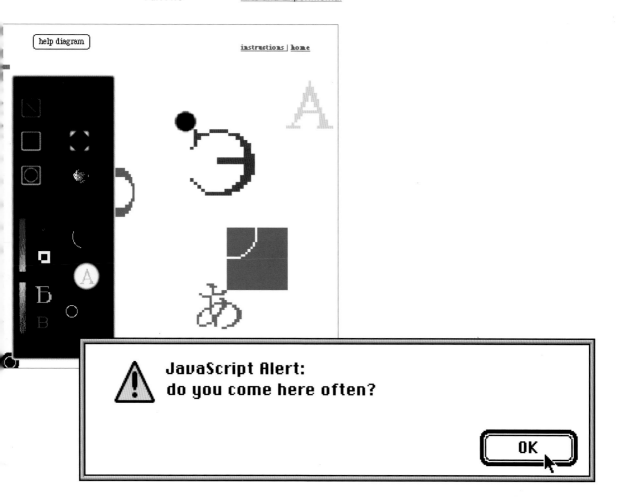

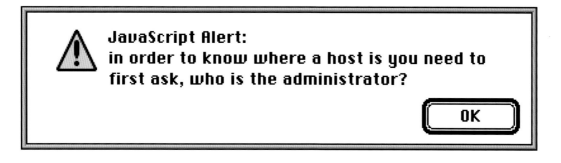

JavaScript Alert:
do you come here often?

OK

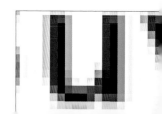

securityland: you are the user, and we are the server

JavaScript Alert:
in order to know where a host is you need to
first ask, who is the administrator?

OK

Art Center College of Design http://www.artcenter.edu The Art Center College of Design Web Art Site, is part of the Alyce de Roulet Williamson Gallery. The work shown here is from a link to the website of Joan Heemskerk and Dirk Paesmans. More from their site is also shown on the next pages.

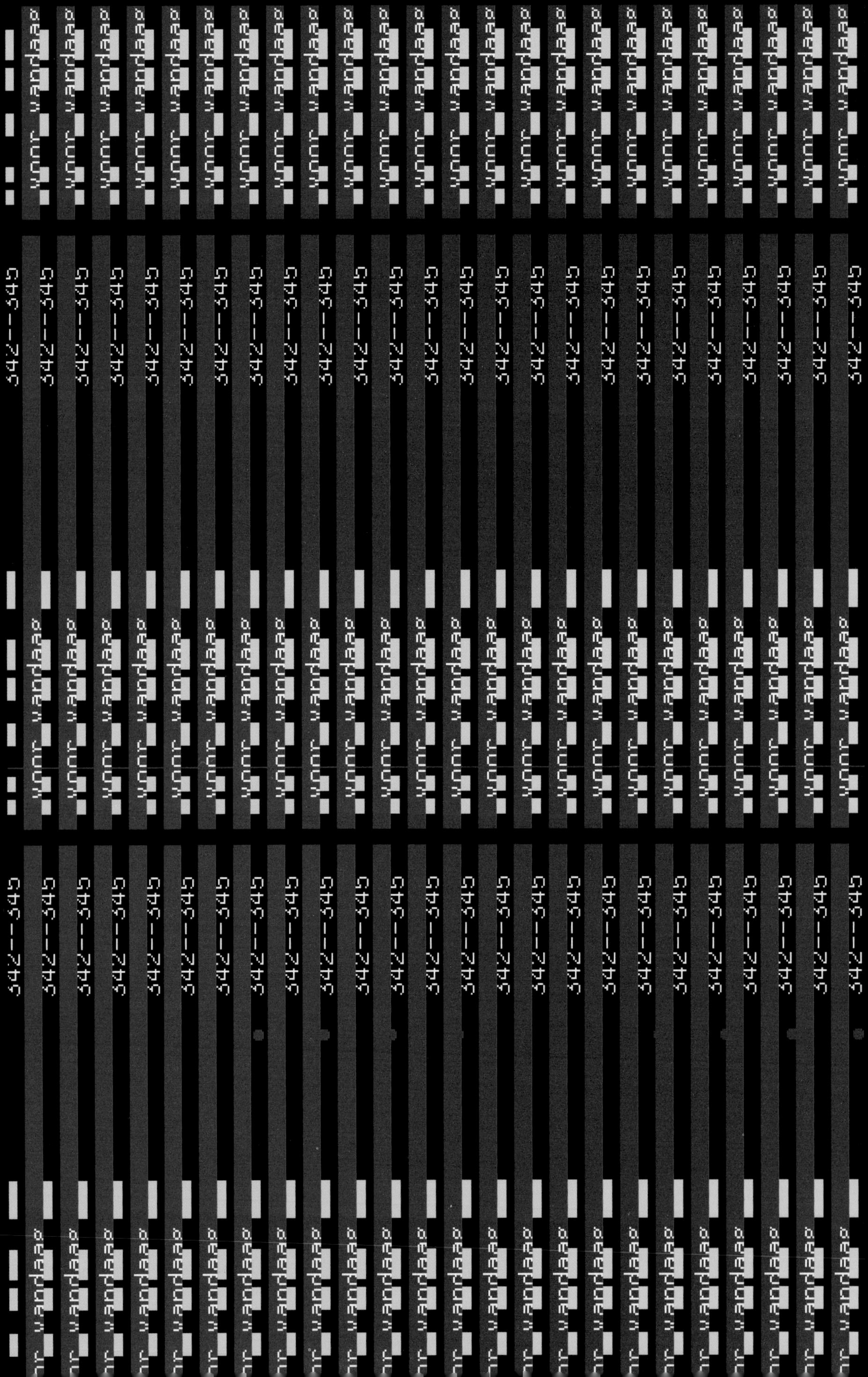

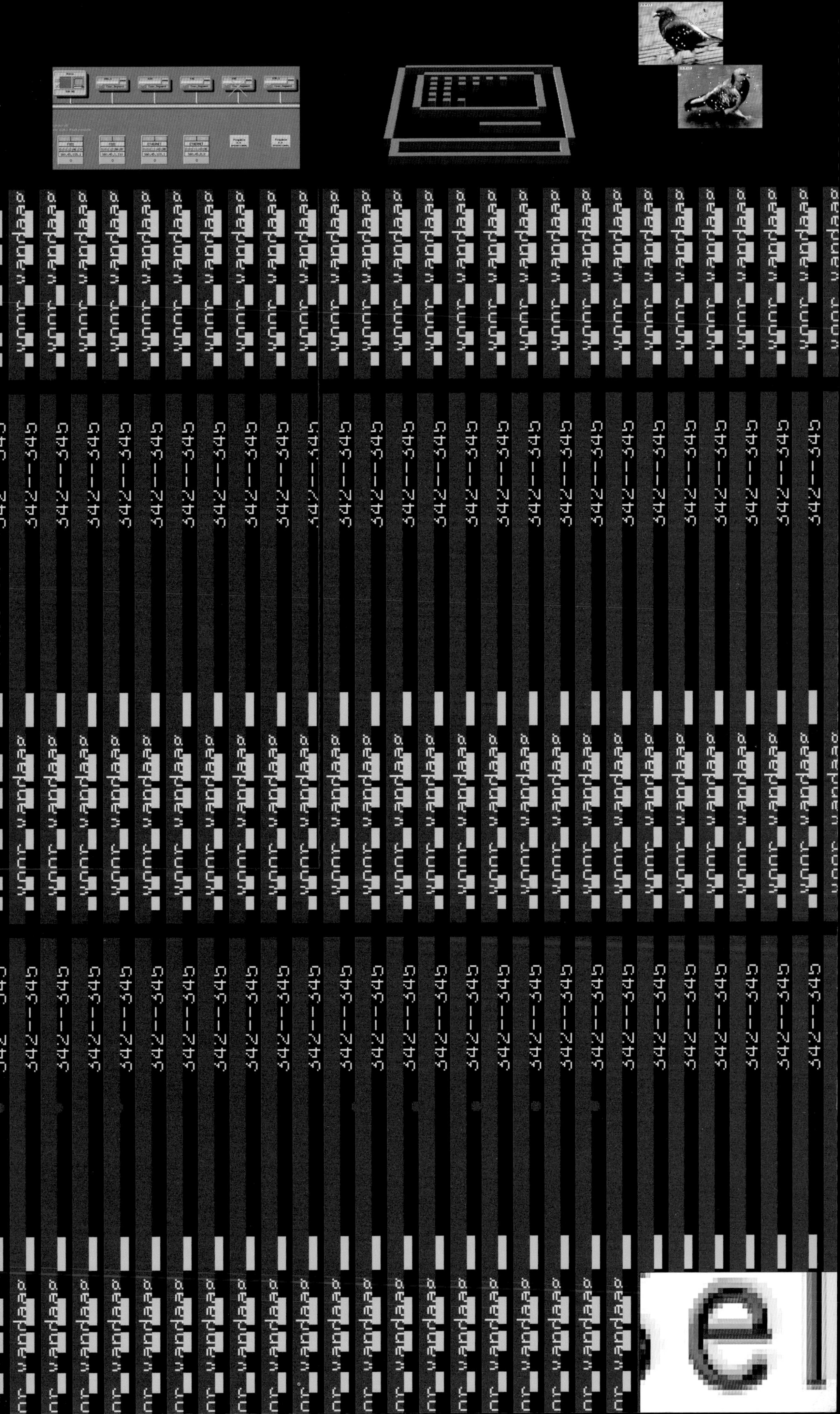
voor_vandaag
342--345

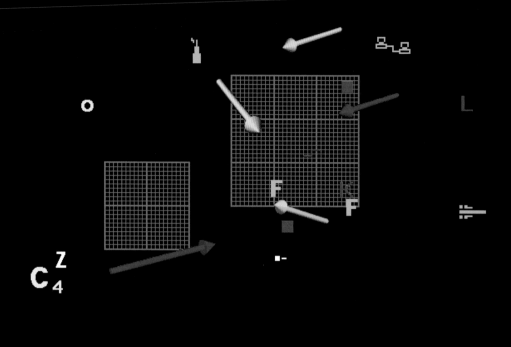

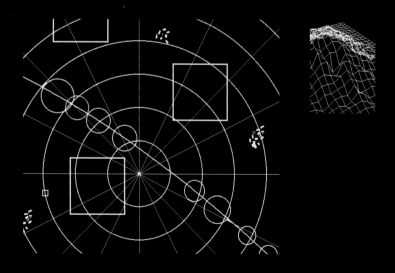

JODI http://www.jodi.org The Web gets deconstructed at this cryptic site.
Team Joan Heemskerk, Dirk Paesmans

```
             }
          } else {
j.set();
j.fill(X, Y, , );
full= true;
       }
   }
(Evt, int x, int y
Mon Jun 23 02:29:1
849398400000

if (resetting) {
return true;
   }
int cellX = x / c
int cellY = y / c
```

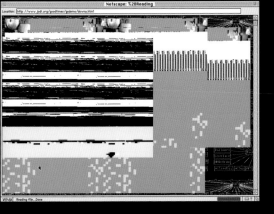

```
private boolean checkMove;
private boolean resetting;
private log
private log[][] =
   {
      }:} _
```

Goodies TM

.SIT

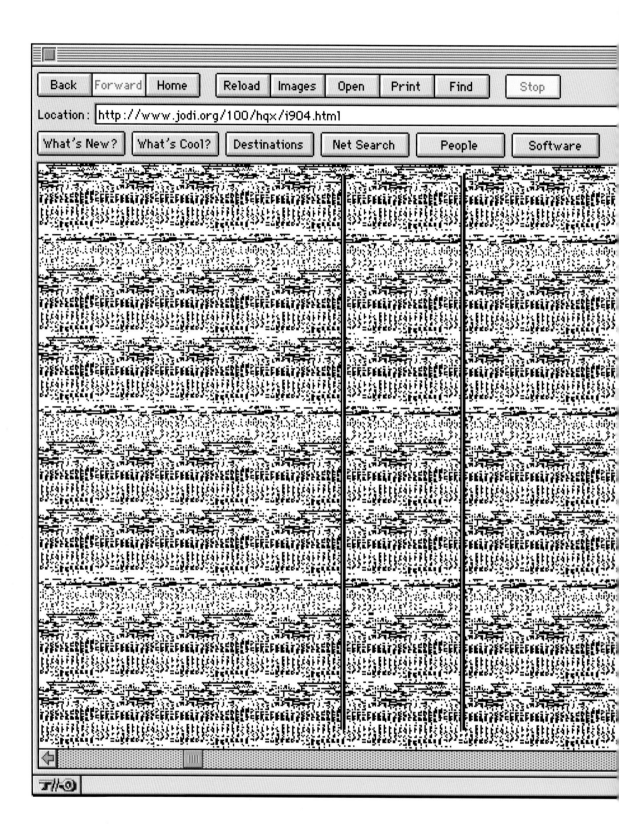

**Netscape: %20View**

● *seize*

[ continue ]  ○ *interviewee*

● *Lynn*  [ Jacksonville ]

● *peddle*
○ *remand*

[ continue ]

| scrooge |
|---------|
| carbuncle |
| AMA |
| gladiator |
| lush |
| intent |
| dine |
| homestead |
| thine |

[ strut ]

| Irwin |
|-------|
| dendrite |
| irate |
| healthy |
| turkey |
| Tom |
| upslope |
| **electroencephalograph** |
| tetravalent |
| muddy |
| rick |
| fragile |
| demon |
| thrush |

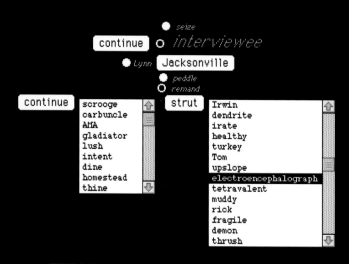

[ vaginal ]  [ continue ]  *continue*

○ *deductible*

[ disposal ]  ● *trisodium*

○ *cobra*  [ continue ]

● *commissariat*

[ patio ]  ○ *Lippincott*

*continue*

| westernmost |
|-------------|
| altercate |
| decelerate |
| butterfat |
| nucleic |
| Lagos |
| phenomenology |
| evict |
| Malcolm |
| recalcitrant |
| hyaline |
| Orlando |
| tat |
| competition |
| corrigenda |
| goldenrod |
| Lola |
| bouquet |
| dearie |

[ salve ]

[ beefsteak ]

| ohm | dying |
|-----|-------|
| Nell | edge |
| kapok | memory |
| beryl | Mel |
| Hickman | Alger |
| bandwagon | sans |
| cedilla | aurora |
| rimy | polarography |
| princess | somehow |
| dystrophy | bat |
| pink | Dixon |
| surpass | another |
| decaffeinate | Atropos |
| bufflehead | Lena |
| irrepressible | flirtatious |
| scriptural | |

[ profess ]

```
0048385041813722316678464425041056885581773
1654061650224651713760756347231307715071014
5806621581347706047456262353467058731881135
0166215662045308777847670671727734566133448
0888667626306187815751327562021010077851582
2111136887325007020131220171673884107707630
3402422663883065748734842741581832285462851
3678537372325176678611816470441820774622055
6744523245253743385225100733880574136461187
5720125342542376376051188660757441463017263
5123400462561232101542015133406110450507764
0882003556672816314424075583458457758224882
2838243768854557027576435660662855871268254
6115233811356126700656547816172883427818044
6574475132781707081875313322377145584118407
5784775661174417885032636746344033411187215
7666562515243100554587010217524302150421056
3774438037148366882305455887854343786780615
5422325631287185151404382183708342685368588
3080142656058242152515202672262671606872687
6130383800112885157848546520317032161452473
7723881731488128537670751323707670178263422
3342881561432756654345435708322766166234377
6533308755281100533311477612001764205171611
7228762174662385486252457640452384362681167
3170576838407248611106478160238657615410460
2051763870358530870637353864344541728126153
1262142871245110565226046273437564880177213
7357823141207472020605585674087723625031252
0103134730325100107832658780052163476861804
5155254287846647008733613323368525881278133
5882683676047471728771370508423012382650464
3234153845326836450473876646112545052446180
7735305880766514636373345882083867418107275
8473221504050843036815424632818766288340845
8412450475000633552430628160016067313352052
0364836467206367484453777240213341745583313
1518014577455606010461216800224375376844681
3620741212430431665142530475276548623754117
1523388442172557734484127873102255585540867
1240185670708782884251846507466601710378360
2585581742700307874675406785256525175360540
6814880566063860226753038300050642231208815
```

Ken Feingold http://www2.sva.edu/ken Artworks by the artist, reports of his
activities and a demonstration of his work for CD-ROM. Studio Ken Feingold
Team Ken Feingold

**Buy**

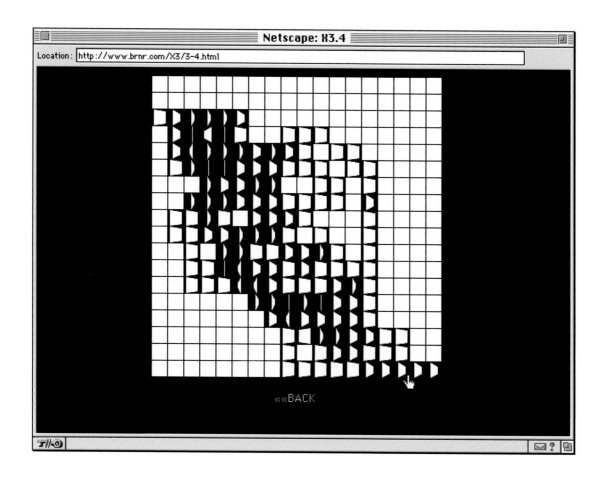

**BRNR** http://www.brnr.com BRNR offers an eclectic mix of graphic
explorations; its content ranges from abstract frames experiments
to nonlinear narrative fiction and light-hearted Shockwave games.
Studio BRNR Graphics Team Michael French

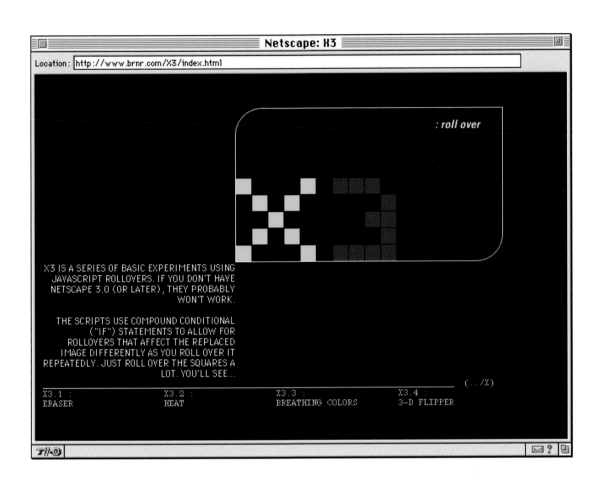

Netscape: X3

Location: http://www.brnr.com/X3/index.html

: roll over

X3 IS A SERIES OF BASIC EXPERIMENTS USING
JAVASCRIPT ROLLOVERS. IF YOU DON'T HAVE
NETSCAPE 3.0 (OR LATER), THEY PROBABLY
WON'T WORK.

THE SCRIPTS USE COMPOUND CONDITIONAL
("IF") STATEMENTS TO ALLOW FOR
ROLLOVERS THAT AFFECT THE REPLACED
IMAGE DIFFERENTLY AS YOU ROLL OVER IT
REPEATEDLY. JUST ROLL OVER THE SQUARES A
LOT. YOU'LL SEE...

( . . /X)

X3.1 :          X3.2 :              X3.3 :               X3.4 :
ERASER          HEAT                BREATHING COLORS     3-D FLIPPER

**Please don't push strangers
in front of oncoming trains**

**Please don't blow the cover
of undercover subway cops**

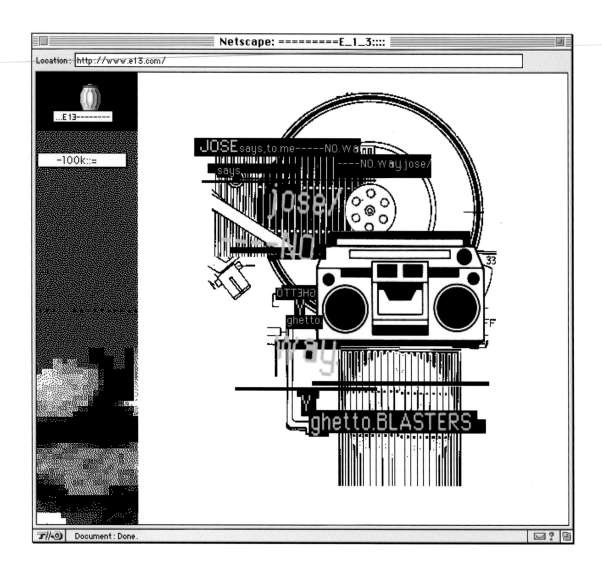

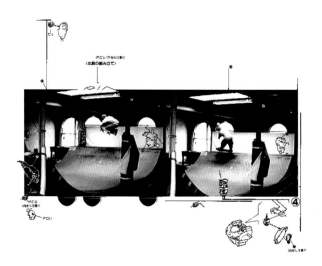

**e13** <u>http://www.e13.com</u> e13 operates as an independent web-zine based on alternative Web design, music, New York City subcultures, new technology and the work of contributors. **Studio** e13 Team Eric Rosevear

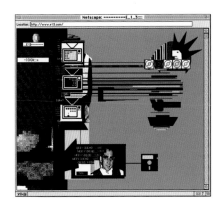

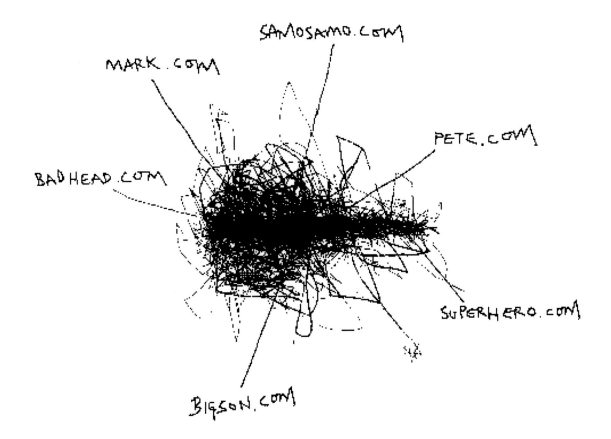

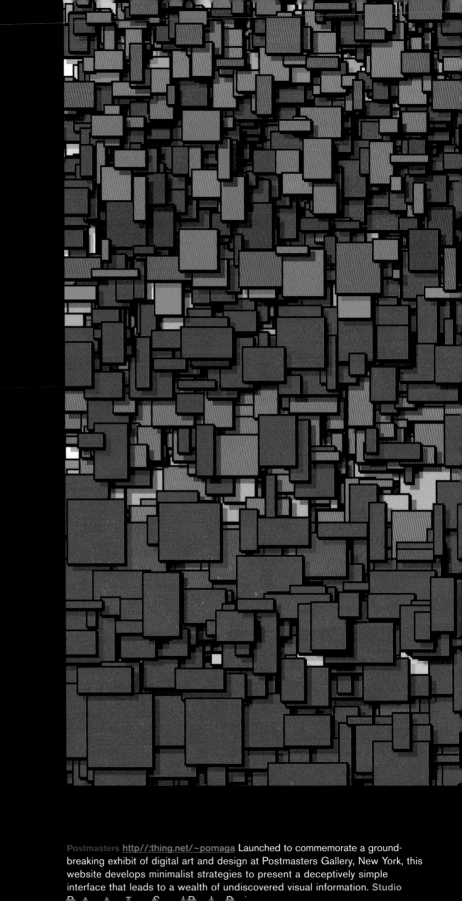

)(

| | | | |
|---|---|---|---|
| 0 | 0 | 0 | 1 |
| 0 | 0 | 1 | 0 |
| 0 | 0 | 1 | 1 |
| 0 | 1 | 0 | 0 |
| 0 | 1 | 0 | 1 |
| 0 | 1 | 1 | 0 |
| 0 | 1 | 1 | 1 |
| 1 | 0 | 0 | 0 |
| 1 | 0 | 0 | 1 |
| 1 | 0 | 1 | 0 |
| 1 | 0 | 1 | 1 |
| 1 | 1 | 0 | 0 |
| 1 | 1 | 0 | 1 |
| 1 | 1 | 1 | 0 |
| 1 | 1 | 1 | 1 |
| 0 | 0 | 0 | 0 |
| 0 | 0 | 0 | 1 |
| 0 | 0 | 1 | 0 |
| 0 | 0 | 1 | 1 |
| 0 | 1 | 0 | 0 |
| 0 | 1 | 0 | 1 |
| 0 | 1 | 1 | 0 |
| 0 | 1 | 1 | 1 |

**Postmasters** http//:thing.net/~pomaga Launched to commemorate a ground-breaking exhibit of digital art and design at Postmasters Gallery, New York, this website develops minimalist strategies to present a deceptively simple interface that leads to a wealth of undiscovered visual information. **Studio**

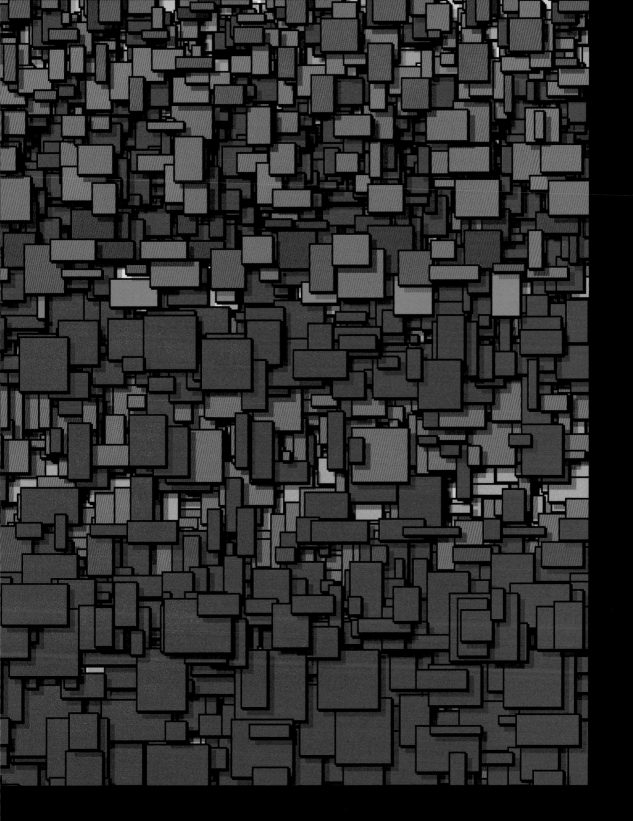

Netscape: Postmasters: Stephen Linhart

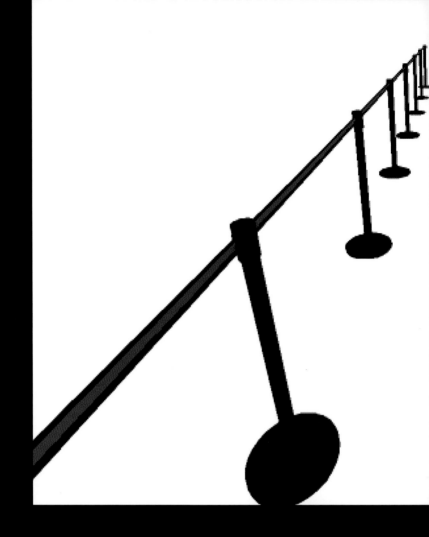

fragments from "Burnt Norton" by T.S.Eliot

Netscape: Postmasters: Craig Kalpakjian

183_

Netscape: Postmasters: Sawad Brooks

Buy

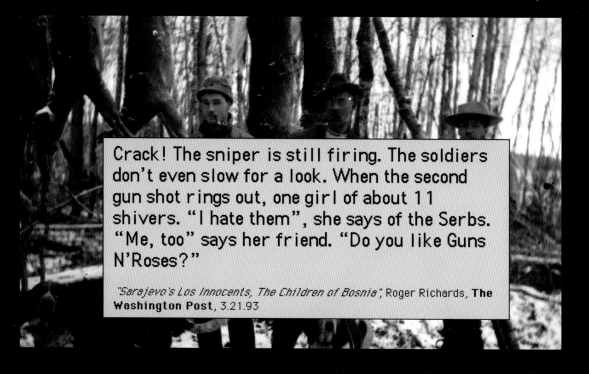

Crack! The sniper is still firing. The soldiers don't even slow for a look. When the second gun shot rings out, one girl of about 11 shivers. "I hate them", she says of the Serbs. "Me, too" says her friend. "Do you like Guns N'Roses?"

*"Sarajevo's Los Innocents, The Children of Bosnia"*, Roger Richards, **The Washington Post**, 3.21.93

Netscape: Postmasters: George Legrady

Physical
Composition

-View
-View
-View
-View
-View
-View
-View
-View
-View
-View

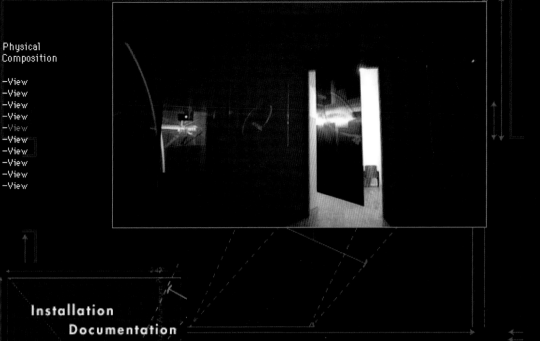

Installation
Documentation

Netscape: Variations on Cryptography

**Grace. Truth. Beauty.**

Cancel    **OK**

Buy

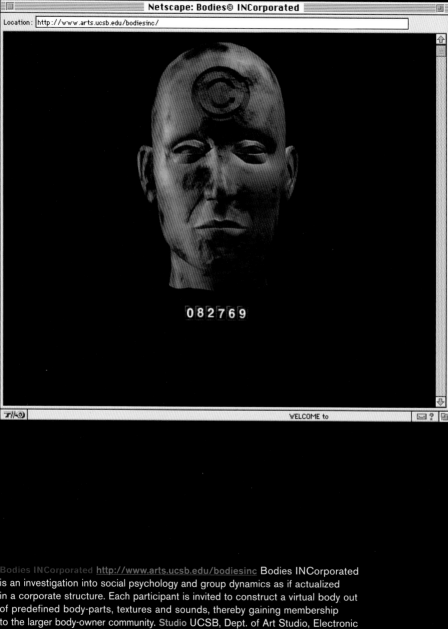

Location: http://www.arts.ucsb.edu/bodiesinc/

082769

WELCOME to

Bodies INCorporated http://www.arts.ucsb.edu/bodiesinc Bodies INCorporated
is an investigation into social psychology and group dynamics as if actualized
in a corporate structure. Each participant is invited to construct a virtual body out
of predefined body-parts, textures and sounds, thereby gaining membership
to the larger body-owner community. Studio UCSB, Dept. of Art Studio, Electronic
Art & Theory (EAT) Lab Team Victoria Vesna, President and CEO (artist/
producer/director); Robert Nideffer, Vice President (artist/writer/html); Nathaniel
Freitas, CTO (vrml/java/cgi programmer); kf.Oe, CAO (composer)

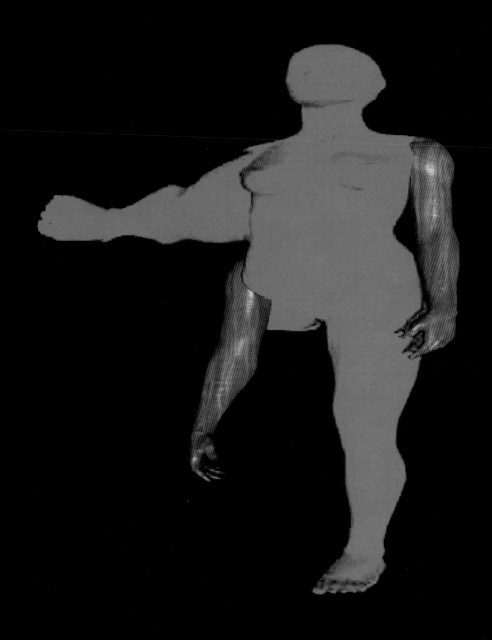

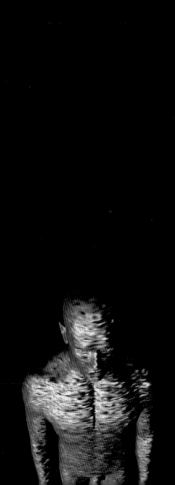

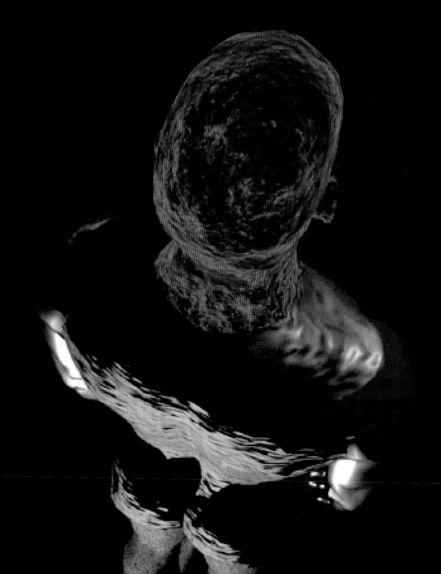

WELCOME to Bodies© INCorporated. The building elements at your disposal are ASCII text, simple geometric forms, TEXTures, and low resolution sound. Bodies built become your personal property, operating in and circulating through public space, free to be downloaded into your private hard drive/communication system at any time. The MOO/WOO functions as an institution through which your body gets shaped in the process of identity construction that occurs in, and mutually implicates, both the symbolic and material realms.

[ continue ]  [ auto setup ]

Sell

Generation X
The Missing Chapter

I pulled the following chapter out of Generation X in April, 1990, the
month I handed it in to my publisher, because it was -- and still is --
too random. The book was published in March, 1991. The narrator is Dag,
telling a bed time story to Claire and Andy.

------------------------------------

"Once upon a time there was a murderer loose in the wheat fields of
Texlahoma, a gruesome murderer who liked to pick on children in
particular, jamming their little limbs into the fan blades of Delta 88's,
and placing vast doses of drugs in their playtime snack cakes -- doses
that would within seconds set their tender little brains like cement.

"So naturally, people were upset, and seniors were doubly worried as the
number of youngsters paying into their social security kitty was
shrinking daily. They screamed for action.

"The concerned folks of Texlahoma therefore met in their local shopping
malls to devise strategies. Their meeting places were the countless
stores left vacant in these malls when the bulk of retail business
collapsed eons ago in the dawn of Texlahoma's history. These stores now
left gaps like missing teeth in between the cheerful greeting card
boutiques and stores selling foamy orange drins. Many other stores had
been converted into senior centers where old folks made felt art and
mobilized as voting blocs. It was in these particular converted stores
where the angry meetings were held.

"'I demand that we organize search parties to hunt for the murderer,'
commanded Senator Blake, the King of Texlahoma who appealed to his
people's finer sentiments, 'and we'll arm these search parties with mace
and handguns and crowbars and stun wands. We'll make our asteroid safe
once more.' Senator Blake had many volunteers and this was good, as the
crimes of the murderer were escalating and he was branching out into
other areas of crime. He was setting fire to fields just before the
harvest. He was blinding whole families at night while they watched TV
game shows by placing flares inside the TV tubes. He was welding shut
the pipes of the sewage treatment facilities which caused backups of
feces and the sawn off digits of murder victims into the bathrooms of
Texlahoma.

"It was all too nasty. When people bumped into each other in the
7-Eleven store to do their shopping," (traditional grocery stores, as
such, don't exist in Texlahoma), "citizens would treat each other with
great mistrust, all the while affecting an air of moral spotlessness
themselves. Bowling leagues dissolved; church attendance became
spasmodic; most everyone ended up staying home at nights watching
reruns, but with a blanket over the screen so they might not be blinded.

"The senior's centers in the malls, meanwhile, became the true social
hot spots as they were the recruiting centers and ammunition depots for
vigilante groups. They also became the clearing house for the latest
tales of terror of the murderer and his gruesome deeds. One night, he
locked a dozen members of a hospital staff in a basement storage room
where he had smashed hundreds of bottles of radioactive isotopes of
iodine, barium and phosphorous. By morning, they were dead of radiation
sickness. Another time he released ten thousand lab rats from a downtown

**Douglas Coupland** http://www.coupland.com The site archives previously
unpublished material by writer and novelist Douglas Coupland, and includes twelve
short stories, video clips of the documentary 'Close Personal Friend' and
MTV spots, the author's personal collection of nuclear test-site photographs, audio
files of readings, and much more **Studio** Sara Bailey **Client** Doug Coupland
and Harper Collins **Team** Douglas Coupland, Art Director; Sara Bailey, Designer;
Graham Law, Programmer

Netscape: Graphis: Eric Adigard

Netscape: Graphis: Michael Cronan

Netscape: Graphis: Amy Franceschini

Netscape: Graphis: David Glaze

Netscape: Graphis: Rodney Alan Greenblat

Netscape: Graphis: Mignon Khargie

Netscape: Graphis: Michael Macrone

Netscape: Graphis: Mark Meadows

Netscape: Graphis: Sara Ortloff

Netscape: Graphis: Fred Sotherland

Netscape: Graphis: Gong Szeto

Netscape: Graphis: John Waters

Buy

**Erik Adigard is co-owner of M.A.D. and the design director for San Francisco-based Wired Digital's Wired News, HotBot, NewBot and LiveWired websites.**

<< **The problem** with graphic design on the Web lies not so much with the Web itself as with the state of graphic design. Originally most graphic designers embraced the computer reluctantly, not for its creative potential but rather because it seemed like the only way to stay in business. A new generation of designers adapted their style to using the Macintosh, but since they were inspired by the production process these remained very incestuous gestures – tons of new typefaces, complex layering of images, 3D, distortions, etc. – that were unrelated to current social trends. Bad design is spreading in our lives because we run too fast toward the future. **With the** Web, you have to forget about the craft of graphic design. You have to place style and sophistication on the back burner and think about methods that have more to do with construction than decoration. The Web was built without regard for what has been learned about design. It became an environment and a culture not because someone designed it, but because people showed up en masse and adopted its values. **The problem** with the Web experience, again, lies not so much with the Web, as with the computer. Computers are simply not ready for the consumer market yet; actually I don't think they are ready for the workplace either. I expect someday to see major class actions against the computer giants like those we are seeing against the tobacco industry. **An experience** is only as good as what you can feel with your body. If the experience of print is imbedded in the multitude of our daily activities – on the plane, in the bathroom, the lobby, the bedroom, the gym, etc. – the desktop experience is physically sedentary and mentally poly-systemic. There is a gap between the experience of the medium and that of the content. The former is bad and the latter is full of variety. **The Web** is superior to any other publishing medium in its ability to exploit connectivity and timeliness. Because there are tremendous possibilities in the Web, there is only one Web but there are as many Web experiences as there are users. Furthermore, the Web is a device for archiving and retrieval of information. It is publishing but it is also utilities – push technologies for instance. With push media, we are getting into a new set of problems. Push media is going to bring the utilities out of the Web; it will customize the Web and make it far easier to consume. A new kind of publishing will come out of it that will be modular and fragmented. **Push media** will bring aggressive marketing to the Web. Big media will certainly dominate this new phase of the Web and perhaps out of it will emerge a new market and a new industry. Push media also represents a new set of possibilities for designers. With the new generation of browsers you can take over the desktop and have a better chance to create a meaningful media experience. **The next** step will be a rethinking of hardware interfaces. The Web will then escape the boundaries of the desktop to appear in new devices, on TV, on beepers, and in public spaces. >>

**Michael Cronan is president and creative director of San Francisco-based Cronan Design, a multi-disciplined firm whose work includes image development, corporate communications, packaging, print graphics, exhibits and art programs. He is also the creative director of Cronan Artefact, a product development, manufacturing and marketing company.** << **Human perception** is

about crossing thresholds. We knit our reality together based on what just happened and what we anticipate is going to happen in the next moment. If you've ever had someone play a really superb practical joke on you, you can remember a moment when your reality went away and suddenly you were left without understanding what the next moment's going to bring, and it's a sickening and kind of delicious feeling at the same time. <u>I think</u> there's a similarity to that many times on the Web. When you can offer somebody an expectation of having, in the next moment, more and better choices, or clearer or more adroit information or instructions, then you've established a kind of engine that can drive someone through a site effectively. Every time somebody makes a choice you want to be able to craft that experience so they have a little reward, as opposed to a little signal that their fun is about to end. <u>Typically what</u> happens on the Internet is that designers make assumptions about what people want to see. They're in a world of the print medium or some sort of slow movie entertainment, they consider the Web as some kind of multimedia experi- ence. In my opinion at this point it's not that. It's more like the case of the little mouse in the cage that hits the endorphin button. When the feedback is a happy or positive response, then the little test subject keeps hitting the same bar. <u>When you</u> can introduce the user to a very positive decision- making choice that feeds them a little about what's expected and a little bit about what's unexpected, and what's unexpected has a positive bent to it, a little more than you anticipated – a little brighter, a little more movement, a little clearer than you anticipated – then you start to train somebody that there's value in this series of thresholds. In that sort of interchange with some- body you're upping your own ante constantly. <u>Most Web</u> designers at this point don't have this kind of interchange in mind when they're designing for people. There are two metaphors I'd use from the Old West, the homestead metaphor and the snake oil metaphor: people are putting their stakes down everywhere and the bottles are beautiful but there's really no content. Sites that have fascinating content are boring to look at, and sites that have very strong graphics have no content. We're all still in the process of lining it up. >>

**Amy Franceschini is widely known for her interface design for San Francisco- based Atlas, the online quarterly magazine. A multimedia artist whose focus is graphic design, she also has her own studio, Future Farmers, specializing in print work, websites and multimedia.** << <u>Right now,</u> the way the Web is, I would think what interests me is a smart interface that arouses your curiosity, one that prompts you. Everything isn't necessarily spelled out for you, but there's enough information to urge you to click on a certain icon or a certain area of the graphic. Only it's not so far out that you don't know what's going on: I like continuity within the insanity. As I've been doing it more and more, I feel like it's just like a big calculus problem and you break it down into little pieces that fit together to make an answer. <u>What's interested</u> me recently is the way the technology is going. Most people who are working on the Web come from a print background and text is really heavy. But in the future, the way we're planning for the way the Web's going to be, the push is not to have text but to have streaming audio and motion video. So I'm interested in pushing towards that direction. The prompts aren't going to necessarily be visual any more. We're going to have to think about things like voice recognition and about what the graphics are going to be to prompt you to ask a question

or tell the computer where to go next. It's going to change our way of thinking.
**I still** love text, but what's interesting to me is to figure out how to use the
combination of text and moving visuals together. I think the people who are
involved in the Web right now aren't really thinking about that. Actually
I'm at a point now where the Web isn't really satisfying me. I do Web design,
and I guess I do it well, but I keep thinking there's got to be more, something
else has to happen. Right now the design and the technology are totally out of
sync. The people in technology are designing things that are just plain
ugly; it's been that way forever. If designers can get in the same lane as the
technology I think things will become more intriguing. **That's why** I'm
getting interested in researching technology more. Five years down the road
everything's going to stream, it's not going to be about waiting for something
to download. It's going to be about real time, and that's what I'm interested in. >>

**David Glaze is creative director of the New Media Group for The Designory,
a Long Beach, California-based studio which helps clients build brands
interactively. He believes that Web developers should always consider communication first and technology second.** << **We prefer** to focus on the value
of interactive content to the end user. It sounds simple, but that's the beauty.
Content should target customers rather than site owners. Visitors have to
become engaged and interested. Web creators need to be very aware of their
audience to successfully encourage people to come, stay and return. You
also have to consider the limitations, as well as the capabilities, of the equipment
your audience is using. **The Designory** has always specialized in long-form
communications, like automobile brochures, which have to organize a lot of information and present it in an engaging format. I think the best way to deliver
so much detail, even the technical details, is to tell a story or create a common
thread that holds everything together. In the corporate world, that thread
is usually the brand, which should be extended across every piece of marketing
communications material, including websites. **It's amazing** how easily the
effectiveness of a corporate website can be diluted. Even the good ones, those
that set out to achieve something specific, can be turned upside down
when you get too many cooks in the kitchen. In a very short time, white papers,
training manuals and all sorts of internal documents of lesser interest to the
consumer start popping up in strange places on the site. The structural integrity
of any site can collapse unless someone stays focused on its purpose
and has the authority to veto any suggestions that are not consistent with the
stated goals and objectives. **Many corporate** officers are now struggling
to measure the value and assess the success of their sites. The big question for
them has become: is our website working? I expect the next wave of sites,
whether new or redesigned, to be driven more by corporate marketing goals than
simply by the need to keep up with the competition. >>

Rodney Alan Greenblat is a New York City-based visual artist and founder of
The Center for Advanced Whimsy. He has published several CD-ROMS,
as well as children's books. << The thing that's missing from CD-ROMs, and
computer games too, is that we don't really have a star system in new media
and the personalities of the makers aren't really that important yet; nobody knows
who wrote them although a lot of really talented people are involved. And
because of that we have this morass of categories of items without people behind
them, although I like to think that's changing. The thing that I really like
about the Web, which I think is different from what business people are saying
about it, is that the great things on it are the personal things, and I think those
work so much better than sites that come from companies, or sites that
are directed towards specific marketing demographics. The people who are just
putting up stuff because they are listening to some inner voice are the ones
who are really doing something different. Or at least they're doing it in a medium
that really suits it; maybe they don't know that. But there's never been
a medium where you can just publish whatever, whenever, and to me that's
really exciting. What's weird is that a lot of companies take an approach
that a website's like a magazine or like a this or a that, but it really isn't.
And so I don't think that approach works so well a lot of the time. Advertising
is an odd thing too, because sometimes it works and sometimes it doesn't.
But I think for the most part the reason much more personal visions really work
on the Web is because you never see them anywhere else. And that's really
exciting to me. >>

Brad Johnson is a designer and partner at Portland, Oregon-based Second
Story Interactive Design (formerly Brad Johnson Presents), which develops
entertainment-oriented interactive projects delivered through disk-based media
and the Web. << One of the most exciting aspects of interactive design is
its rapid evolution. There is a mood of acceleration and speed that penetrates the
entire industry, and its constant redefinition of itself makes for a challenging
career. Our creative tools become more powerful, there is greater breadth to our
expressive range, our audiences grow larger, and the nature of the experiences we create for them is never the same. While our medium is continually
reinventing itself, so are we reinventing ourselves as designers. While the
technical constraints associated with working on floppy disk-based projects once
seemed severely limiting, creating content on the Internet was another few
giant steps backward. But even though the Web seemed to take the 'multi' out of
multimedia, there was one strength it had that outweighed everything else:
distribution. Anyone in the world had instant access to your content regardless
of their platform. The Web's limited bandwidth, its early lack of media
integration and its inadequate layout control leveled the playing field for everyone
involved. The excitement was in finding creative possibilities within the strict
confines of the limited technology: ironically, there was something liberating for
me in those tight parameters. As the browsers evolved and modems got
faster, a site's complexity grew — and so did the teams. As Web technologies
continue to evolve, so must the nature of the interactive design firm. With
the ever increasing creative possibilities unfolding before us, Brad Johnson
Presents has itself transformed: with my partner Julie Beeler, I founded

Second Story, which continues to develop content-driven, entertainment-oriented websites. Our work has always been focused on 'telling the story,' and as creators in an interactive medium, we feel our role is to bring another dimension to the content, which is to say, our job is "to tell the second story." >>

**Mignon Khargie is design director of Salon, the San Francisco-based daily online literary magazine that recently was awarded Time's Best Web Site of the Year.** << <u>For me,</u> one of the biggest differences between designing a page meant for print and designing a page which will live only in the computer has been in the tools I now use. The fundamental problem of information delivery remains the same for both forms of media: we're all trying to find a creative way to tell our stories. It may seem an easier problem to solve in print, since there you don't have to worry about holding the reader's attention for the duration of yet another mouse-click followed by downloading time. But solutions in the online world are multi-dimensional, and given the rate at which technology is evolving, it would seem as though your only limit is the extent of your imagination. <u>The distance</u> between designer and reader also seems to have been shortened, and is now measurable by the length of time it takes to send e-mail to a bulletin board or a mailbox. Reader feedback is immediate and makes up for a lack of physical presence with loud personality. There are few timid people on the Internet: they all have something to say, and they all get to say it. Designing in this environment can be a daily dose of gratification, or a smack in the face. Readers will let you know quickly what they do not like. <u>This is</u> an industry where we are all teaching each other and learning from each other, where no one person can possibly know all the intricacies of Web publishing, and where designers need to work in tandem with programmers. At Salon, everyone is in charge of their own sections, since not only does it makes a difference in our work if we feel some ownership in what we do, but in many ways it's becoming harder to split tasks: the best interfaces are built by designers who are close to the material and able to focus clearly on the design issues. Keeping an eye on the overall picture is a job which is definitely getting to be more complex with each layer of change in technology. >>

**Michael Macrone is the webmaster for Atlas magazine and one of its co-founders. He is also the author of best-selling guidebooks to the classics, including Brush Up Your Poetry and his most recent, Naughty Shakespeare.** << <u>The pitfall</u> of the Web, and the beauty of it at the same time, is that all kinds of people who are completely incompetent are doing it. There are a lot of sites out there that have good design but are lacking in content, although I don't like those terms to much. If it's good it's good, if it's not, it's not. It's a question of how well it's done. There's been a false dichotomy since the very beginning when people talk about the Web. They tend to talk about it either as eye candy or hard information. If it's an informative site you can expect it to be ugly, if it's a beautiful site you can expect it to be empty. But after all, beauty itself is a kind of content, isn't it? <u>What we're</u> trying to do with Atlas is conquer the divide, to have something that has content and is compelling and also looks good. There are principles we're learning about as we go along: keeping the design as simple as possible, making sure that the user isn't overwhelmed, giving them a chance to find their way to the story they want to hear and then guiding them through the story so they can always get out, or get back, or find what they're

looking for. And that's a tall order when you're dealing with a long story, and I'm not sure we have yet to come up with a good solution. **I'd say** the ideal design for a website is a pyramid in form. You start at a relatively small point that gives you a small number of choices and of those choices, each will reveal a little more to you or get you into a more specialized branch of the tree, and once you're on that branch you start getting to smaller branches. **Given the** massive amount of content on a highly developed, long-running website, designers are having to start to figure out how much a user can absorb. It's different from newspaper or television, yet there are no guidelines. It's a feedback mechanism of some kind. You're learning how to provide ways of experiencing the site and reacting to it. You have to train the user to use your site, you have to modify their behavior to some degree. But you have to take for granted that everybody has a common baseline you can use. **Users also** train themselves. There are areas of the screen they learn to look at, areas that they ignore. The human brain is constantly struggling to block out stimulation and data. They ignore the ads, they ignore the navigation unless they need it. Everybody talks about the overwhelming overload of information and they're right; it's like being in Times Square the way these websites just throw everything but the kitchen sink at you, and yet people learn to deal with that. >>

**Mark Meadows is Chief Investigative Officer and one of the founders of Construct, a San Francisco-based studio that designs virtual environments.**
<< **What really** attracted to me to digital design was the level of innovation that's expected from you. Digital media, because it's able to assimilate so fast, stays very interesting. Whereas before a design movement might last for several decades, now things can change in a matter of weeks. That everything is going in such radical directions is really exciting. At the same time I find it vaguely frustrating because I think there's a level of depth that isn't being addressed. **I'm really** interested in seeing a cyberspace that is a collage of a lot of different media types, one that is being manipulated on a very deep level by the people who are participating in and contributing to it. I see a much more random non-designed environment. I don't think cyberspace should look designed any more than a city street does. I also think that eventually computers will be doing the design for us. **There are** two basic visual elements involved: color and line. Desktop publishing heavily influenced the way in which both of these elements were introduced to the design world. Colors were very bright and often had a low saturation level, or in some cases a very high saturation level. I think what people noticed was they were looking at different colors on the monitor than what they had generally been used to in print. You're looking at light instead of staring at reflected light. Also, everyone was trying to get a very clean line going, but the medium itself is not conducive to that. So why keep trying for the clean line and the beveled edge? Let's push things in a rougher direction. **Layout is** a completely different department. Our approach is in the direction of randomization. Looking at what the media is really good for, if you can get away from preconceived notions about what

design and layout is supposed to be and find out what the Web is best at and try
to exploit those particulars I think you've ended up with a stronger design role.
It's still so very early. It takes decades for a medium to really figure out what its
voice is. My hunch this week is that there's going to be a much more intense
integration with the real world. That's something I'm personally very interested in
seeing, having location-based entertainment that is in some ways connected
to the Internet. I don't think the Internet as something like interactive television is
going to be interesting enough for people. We need to get more of our
bodies into it. It just seems to me natural. The most dissatisfying thing about the
Internet is how it is so unattached to the world. In some ways that's also
something that's really fascinating. >>

**Sara Ortloff is the design director of San Francisco-based Ikonic. Inc, coordinating
strategic corporate planning with the senior management group representing
the design community.** << I think what is really different about design online is
that you have the opportunity to work collaboratively with your client and
team members to build a holistic experience, a kind of brand extension that isn't
possible in other interactive environments such as CD-ROMs or kiosks,
which can be terribly static. The Web is always changing. I think the Web is very
similar to our experience of physical reality, although the major difference
is that people don't take anything in without making a choice to do so. So when
you're building websites you need to be very acutely aware of how every
decision you make about functionality, features, content, and look are all driving
towards supporting the filter of what the brand is trying to communicate
and deliver to the customer. The real excitement for me is building relationships
with people by providing them with relevant information as opposed to
merely all the information. That should all be completely transparent to the users.
They shouldn't be preoccupied with how the relevance is being delivered;
they should see it as an attribute of the brand. Users should be able to make
a choice and then the information that comes back to them is not only
useful but it's somehow personalized. It's somehow relevant to who the user is,
as opposed to who the next person is on the client side of the server. So if
people show a continued interest in a certain area of content or activity they start
getting those areas fed to them in some other more aggressive way, because
the website knows what they're interested in. The brand response is relevance
as opposed to randomness. I think that's a real migration in website
design from a few years ago when everyone was trying to get a site up with
content that was re-purposed from whatever collateral their clients had on hand.
There is a real challenge with technology like push media not to bombard
people with random 'floaters' across their desktop. But if it's used very prudently,
it is potentially one of the major innovations on the Web, and one that will
transform the whole experience. >>

**Fred Sotherland is senior vice-president and creative director for San
Francisco-based CNET: The Computer Network.** << _When we_ launched CNET

we came in with the lowest common denominator, somebody with 216
Web colors and a 14.4 modem on a 640x480 screen, and two years later it
really hasn't changed. We started out with a page limit of 20K but we've
slowly been cheating on that and we're realizing we've been cheating too much.
We're trying to get below 20K, to figure out ways to have a page with
little or no graphics but still have a unique look and feel, and that's a huge
challenge right now. _The issue_ going forward is that there are not only
multiple ways of displaying information on what we're calling the Web right now,
but there's also going to be multiple speeds at which people come in.
I think this low bandwidth is going to be with us for many years to come, in the
form of wireless communication. You have to figure out how to deliver
your content both ways, for a high- and low-bandwidth audience. The content
is going to remain the same but the design is definitely going to diverge.
_Right now_ everybody's in search of the ultimate interface to disseminate information. If somebody's doing something good, other companies will try
to follow suit and then all of a sudden a standard trend tends to develop. In a
perfect world, I'd love for everybody to get together on an interface so
that a user doesn't have to figure out a whole new paradigm at each new website.
_The perfect_ interface should generically appear and you could put your
own look and feel to it, but consumers could then navigate any website they
got to. Not having a common interface language makes it really difficult
for consumers to follow on the Web. I think that's something huge that is lacking
right now. _I think_ the next thing on the horizon is offline browsing, but
it's an odd concept because the whole idea of the Web is that it's a live, ever-
changing medium that's constantly updated with news and information.
Offline browsing brings you a richer, more multimedia experience but it does it
at the cost of immediacy. _The other_ issue is browser wars. With two major
standards and all the upgrades, it's taking more and more resources to design
a Web page. We just keep amassing different versions we have to build
for; there really isn't any other medium like that. It doesn't fit any kind of business
model for being able to design that way. >>


**Gong Szeto is a creative partner in, and one of the four founders of io.360,
a New York-based design studio whose output is entirely for online media.**
<< _We are_ very attracted to the jury-rigged aspects of today's technology. There

are a lot more uncertainties that arise than in traditional print design; we
see them as opportunities. The fragile and indeterminate nature of the medium
has some really exciting aspects to it. It opens up an arena where much of
what the designer thinks about and designs is not even visual — it's in the flow,
in the structure, in the relationships of discrete parts. _While working_ with
databases, the designer has to think in a predictive way about how the application is going to be used, where an invisible user is asking for certain kinds of
information. So interfaces or Web pages that are built on the fly have to be generated from a set of rules the designer comes up with. I think a lot of the
determinism is removed from the equation as a result, and the designer has to
learn how to design in an indeterminate system, considering factors like

scalability and extensibility in a computational rather than paper-based way. And
that's a fairly new, very radical thing, I think, for a lot of designers. <u>With all</u>
of that in mind I think our responsibility as designers is to be found in the classi-
cal functions of architecture; namely, to provide a set of solutions that is going
to have firmness (meaning it has to have a solid rationale), commodity (accommodate the needs of the client and the end user) and delight (why offend?).
<u>We like</u> the democratic properties of the medium, its mass accessibility. In many
ways design can be viewed as a very elitist commodity; but in the free-for-all
of the Web, if you can buy your way into having access you have access to anything. We like the idea of a very open and nonspecific audience that's going
to be enjoying our work, rather than targeting any specific segment of society. >>

**John Waters is president and creative director of New York-based Waters Design**
**Associates Inc** << <u>I think</u> there are three points worth mentioning: <u>First,</u> we've
been surprised to find that Web-related work – Internet or intranet site architecture and its design and implementation – now accounts for 60 percent of our
business. We are also using the Web as a presentation and collaboration tool, even
on non-Web projects. <u>Second,</u> our own website is an important marketing
tool – we use it to show some of our work, some of our clients, and some of our
approach – and as an experimental playground, to test new applications,
programming, etc. We also use it as a tool for collaboration between our designers,
programmers, illustrators and clients. <u>Third,</u> we hear a lot about the isolation
imposed by the computer. Balancing solitary and group time has always been
a problem. We all need a degree of time alone, but in business today,
we need one another more than ever. As more data becomes information
and information becomes knowledge we realize that individuals cannot handle
it all alone. We require specialists in different areas. But more than that
we need a way for specialists to work together. Complexity demands
collaboration. For that reason I think the Web is one of the best collaborative
tools available today. >>

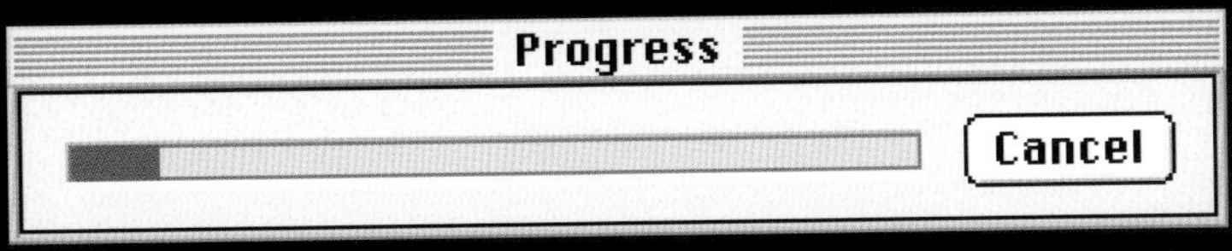

**Progress**

Cancel

**äda'web** 32 West 22nd Street, New York, NY 10010 212.620.7288 (ainatte@adaweb.com)   8_
http://www.adaweb.com Since Fall 1994 Target Unanticipated 'viewsers' (viewers/users) who enjoy   9_
play, appreciate the unexpected, relish the medium's contradictions, and prefer the unusual   161_
pursuit over instant gratification Traffic 28,000 hits per day, 17,000 visits per month Awards Entertain-   163_
ment Weekly Top Ten Multimedia Products Webby Award, Cool Site of the Day. **Adaweb** is a   164_
curated site that produces cultural content specifically for the Web. The approach is unusual in that   165_
both the work process and the projects themselves are a collaboration, redefining the concept   166_
of authorship. The site is a 'digital foundry' for artists, musicians, architects, writers, filmmakers and   167_
others who do not necessarily have prior Web experience. They work closely with staff designers
and programmers to produce projects that use the Web as a new medium, and not just as a new venue
or distribution model. Using a plethora of media, the site focuses on the distinctive aspect of the
medium — i.e. the network of information. **Focusing** on networkship, Adaweb encourages institutional
partners, a participatory experience, and the fusion of the online world with the 'real' one. Instead of
relegating the context of our endeavor to the periphery, we chose to imbed it as the fulcrum of our work.
Jenny Holzer http://www.adaweb.com/project/holzer David Bartel http://www.adaweb.com/partners
Vivian Selbo http://www.adaweb.com/project/selbo GroupZ http://www.adaweb.com/project/~GroupZ
Tools Pen and paper, Photoshop, Illustrator, BBEdit, DeBabelizer, GifBuilder, Netscape,
Fetch, Director, AppletAce, Cinemac, SoundEdit 16, Palace, QuarkXPress, Transparency, WEBmap

**Adjacency: Brand New Media™** 2020 17th Street, San Francisco, CA 94103 415.487.4510   136_
(info@adj.com) http://www.adjacency.com Rollerblade http://www.rollerblade.com Since July 1996
Target Inline skaters of all brand allegiances Traffic 7,500 distinct hosts per week. **Adjacency**
designed the site at a time when the clients were reconsidering and refining their brand direction.
We knew that whatever we came up with couldn't be too over-stylized because the look of
Rollerblade was about to be redefined. We decided that to create a piece that would be still be relevant
later we needed to focus on the action and look of the activity of inline skating. Inline skating-
related Web sites at the time tended to look like publications, with small, inset rectangular photos and
itty-bitty product shots taken from the profile. We wanted to counter that. We decided to go for
a large look with type contoured to the composition of the photos and where possible, reinforcing any
motion in the shot. We wanted to create big, deep pages that fetishized the products. Tools Apple
Power Macs, Photoshop, Illustrator, BBEdit and Quick Keys

**Primo Angeli Inc** 590 Folsom Street, San Francisco, CA 94105 415.974.6100 (rmedeiros@primo.com)   58_
http://www.primo.com Since January 1995 Target Business to business Traffic 50 visitors a day   59_
Awards 1996 Mobius Award for Outstanding Creativity **We evolved** naturally and full-force into website
design. It was a comfortable, natural progression that grew out of our effectiveness in branding,
packaging and print work, and our complete immersion and considerable investment in high-tech
equipment. As architects of many brand and package programs, we construct identities and
messages in areas with very little real estate. Tools Photoshop, Illustrator, SiteMill, GifBuilder, Netscape

**Robert Appleton** 250 8th Avenue, Suite 4S, New York, NY 10011 212.633.7599 (bebopple@interport.net)   3_
http://www.robertappleton.com Since 1997 Target People **This is** a place where I show   186_
projects developed for various media, including, but not limited to, the Web. Tools All media translated   187_
by or created on Macintosh computers and an Agfa scanner with Photoshop, Illustrator,   193_
Director, QuarkXpress, GifBuilder, Netscape and HTML   203_

**Art Center College of Design** 1700 Lida Street, Pasadena, CA 91103 818.396.2379 (sfrolick@artcenter.edu)   120_
http://www.artcenter.edu Since November 1995 Target potential applicants to the college,   121_
aged 18-23 years old, as well as all others interested in the college and its programs Traffic Hundreds   122_
of thousands of visitors in the past year Awards High Five **The dynamism** of the Web is a key   123_
factor in our enthusiasm for this new media: the Web makes typography and imagery kinetic. Text isn't   168_
passive here — it's activated. People tend to view text on the Web as 'pure information,' not as   169_
typographic information; there seems to be a consensus that the Web has finally emancipated the word
from the designer's hand. But we think this notion of freedom is limited. It's limited by default type
options and the Web's origins as a text-based medium. We've chosen to circumvent these limitations,
not out of any 'designer conceit' or arrogance but, rather, to expand the visual language of the
Web. In our site we have treated HTML text as image to blur the notion that it is pure information and
to explore the richness of an information space beyond the perceived purity of its surface.

Art Center's site can be navigated both textually and spatially. While viewing samples of student work on the portfolio screen, visitors may click directly on hazy images layered in the background to call them up for a closer look. The ability to explore the site visually and experientially gives it a distinctive presence on the Web, where text-heavy sites are still the norm. Rather than merely scanning the screen's surface, viewers have the experience of moving deeper into the site, much as they would a physical space. By clicking on a tiny ochre dot that appears on each of the site's 400 screens, visitors are led to a textual map of the entire site, complete with requisite 'You Are Here' indicator. They may actually browse through the virtual college now laid out before them. Subsequent phases of the site will provide access to information about alumni relations, special events, development, and financial aid. Community space for students, faculty, and prospective students will be online as well. Tools Power Macintosh, Illustrator, Photoshop, QuarkXpress, Streamline, BBEdit, WebStar

**Atlas Web Design** 1201B Howard Street, San Francisco, CA 94103 415.553.4074 (olivier@sirius.com) http://www.atlasmagazine.com Since August 1995 Target The broadest possible audience Traffic 25000 to 30000 hits per day Awards Cool Site of the Day, Microsoft Network Site of the Week, The Net Magazine Top 100 Sites, Webby Award. Atlas was judged one of the ten best-designed websites of 1996 by Communication Arts and was selected for content, interface, and design as one of the top 30 independent Web sites shown at IndieNet 96. The site is in the permanent collection of the San Francisco Museum of Modern Art. Atlas Magazine is an unusual site in that it combines top design with exceptional content – documentary photography, multimedia, animation, illustration and new media. That in itself is a great challenge, as well as finding the time and willing contributors with enough talent to keep Atlas interesting and innovative. Atlas was originally conceived as a collaborative effort to create a site which reflected the abilities and talents of its creators and contributors to their fullest, without limiting them to advertorial or editorial guidelines which so often dilutes the quality and impact of a publication. Putting an issue of Atlas together is always a major challenge in that we need to utilize the technology of the day to make the content and design work seamlessly. This process seems to take longer and longer as the Internet develops and our viewers become more and more savvy about the choices available to them elsewhere. We would like to believe that most people are curious about technology, design and content and how these elements can be married effectively on the Internet, and that Atlas can satisfy that need. Tools Photoshop, Illustrator, BBEdit, Sitemill, Gifmation, Director Butler, Shine & Stern Inc http://www.bsands.com Since April 1997 Target Clients, prospective clients, prospective employees, advertising and marketing communities. What's unusual and even, dare we say, unique about the site is its elegant design style, coupled with a good sense of humor. The company logo is of a couple of wrestlers and a referee; we animated it so they're beating each other up, while the ref blows his whistle. The dog page is one of the highlights. Otis, the German Shepherd, leads both QuickTime VR tours of the firm's offices. Tools BBEdit, Photoshop, Illustrator, Sitemill, Gifmation, Director

**Aufuldish & Warinner** 183 The Alameda, San Anselmo, CA, 94960 415.721.7921 (aufwar@aol.com) fontBoy http://www.well.com/user/bobauf/fontboy.html Since September 1996 Target Graphic designers and people who like odd type Traffic 100-200 hits per day fontBoy addresses the problem of keeping a simple, low-maintenance presence on the Internet to avoid the costs and complexities associated with printing and distributing paper-based catalogs. The website allows visitors to view the fontBoy library of fonts in both character and text settings. Pages are devoted to special characters, swell features, and the newest release. Licensing information and an order form are also included. Although fontBoy's motto is "Baroque modernism for the new millennium," the site is designed for maximum clarity and speed of transfer, relying on the personality of the fonts and decorative material to lend uniqueness. The imagery and interface elements were purposefully kept simple enough to ensure that they download quickly. fontBoy hates the World Wide Wait. Tools Macintosh; Illustrator, Photoshop, Simple Text, Netscape

88_
89_
90_
91_
92_
93_
148_
149_

66_
67_
68_
69_

**Sara Bailey** 2320 Woodland Drive, No. 3, Vancouver, BC V5N3P2, Canada 604.879.3301 192_
(bailey@eciad.bc.ca) http://www.eciad.bc.ca/~sbailey/home/ Douglas Coupland http://www.coupland.com
Since May 1996 Target Readers of Douglas Coupland's books and his fans What was refreshing
about making this site is that Doug came to the project with a strong visual sense of how it should
look (collages, imagery, etc.) though he had never had any experience with Web design. I took
his direction and adapted it to the Web though I knew we were pushing the audience boundaries by
making the site so image-heavy. Doug wanted to present his fans with a collection of unpublished
material to discover and peruse, therefore user-centered navigation was not the solution; we wanted
the audience to explore the site and not know where they were headed. The overall idea was
to make the site itself a work of art and to ignore the typical conventions of most Web sites.

**BBC Internet Services** Room G362, BBC White City, 201 Wood Lane, London W12 7TS 0181.752.4476 118_
(dominik@malaise.com) http://www.bbc.co.uk Since November 1993 Target The BBC's 119_
radio and TV audience Traffic Between 3-5 million hits per week Tools The BBC does not endorse
specific software tools

**BRNR Graphics** 304 Mulberry Street, Suite 4H, New York, NY 10012 212.925.2421 (mfrench@brnr.com) 176_
http://www.brnr.com Since January 1997 Target designers or those interested in Web design, 177_
people with interests similar to my own Awards Speared Peanut BRNR is a design-driven site. It was
initially created as a place for me to adapt my own visual vocabulary to digital media, and so in
a small way I have tended to consider the design itself to be content. A singular concern I've had with
design on the Web – and something that has consequently affected much of what I've done
with BRNR – is what sometimes appears to be a general intolerance for subtlety in structure and
navigation online. Obviously, there are certain types of information which lend themselves to subtlety
and others that do not, and there are sites which work well on both ends of the spectrum – but
sometimes Web designers behave as if it is taboo to deviate from very predictable, orthodox
navigation and interaction. That very little of the content on BRNR is prefaced with any kind of expla-
nation, disclaimer, or synopsis is probably a reflection of my own penchant for discovery through
experimentation and exploration, and the fact that BRNR's content is mostly just entertainment allows
me to take such navigational liberties. So even though I sometimes have serious commentary
that I'd like to convey, I find it helpful to wrap that commentary in (often playful) visual iconography,
and let the viewer extract his or her own text. Tools Photoshop, BBEdit, DeBabelizer, GifBuilder,
Director, Freehand, and a sketchbook

**The Center for Advanced Whimsy** 61 Crosby Street, New York, NY 10012 212.219.0342 (rodney@ 40_
whimsyload.com) http://www.whimsyload.com Since Halloween 1996 Target Kooky artists 41_
and tweenagers Traffic I don't want to know Awards New York's 50 Most Fun Sites (New York Now) 42_
How does this site reflect the goals and philosophy of its creators? It is our philosophy. Our 43_
mission is, of course, to spread silliness and promote the inexplicable. We will prove intelligent goofiness
exists, and meaningful ideas that can change the world will be gift-wrapped in playful cartoon
abandon. In that way seriousness and mediocrity might just be overcome after all. The Cartoon
Revolution will begin, ushering in 1000 years of Saturday mornings, where people will get up
when they want to, eat colorful breakfast cereal, and do their work for fun. It will be a future unknown
to corporate advertising departments. What technical hurdles did you have to overcome? We have
yet to overcome any of them. Tools Photoshop, PageMill, Painter, BBEdit, DeBabelizer, Freehand,
Director, Shockwave, Quicktime, Midi

**CNET: The Computer Network** 150 Chestnut Street, San Francisco, CA 94111 415.395.7800 106_
(info@cnet.com) http://www.cnet.com Since June 1995 Target Computer and technology enthusiasts 107_
Traffic CNET is rated the number-one online network serving computer and technology
enthusiasts Awards Marketing Computers ICON Award, Optima Design Award, Newmedia Invision
Award (finalist), Marketing Computers ICON Award CNET's network of websites are designed
to provide our viewers with the latest, up-to-date news and information on computers and technology.
Because we reach such a wide variety of readers, we design our websites to load as fast as
possible, eliminating the need for unnecessary plugins. Some animation has been done using Shockwave
and Javascript, however we try to have a clean build to send out to the majority of our readers.

**We have** deferred using frame tags, for example, because we have determined that this technology requires a longer download time. We studied the time it takes to access certain table structures, and have tried to speed up the user experience as much as possible. Our pages use a Netscape 216-color palette, and we limit the page to 18k of graphics in a 640x480 screen. Tools Illustrator, Photoshop, and HTML editors

**Construct Internet Design** 448 Bryant Street, San Francisco, CA 94107 415.357.0100 (texter@construct.net) http://www.construct.net Since June 1999 Traffic 40,000 hits per day Target revolutionaries, reactionaries, adventuristic capitalists, excommunicated socialists, sympathetic Luddites, hi-tech industry leaders, keiretsu, visionaries, the criminal element, rhetoreticians, impression-able youth, even more impressionable press, skeptical spinsters, virtual architects, inflatable architects, disassembled cyborgs, naturalists, unidentified avatars, unwed teenage mothers and devout atheists. Awards Stolichnaya Electronic Art Award 1996 **The site** does not conform to standard interface design rules. It is nonlinear and marginally chaotic, a reflection of the interdisciplinary spectrum of education and experience integrated in the body construct. The site itself is something of an organic entity; growing in starts and spurts, constantly changing to accommodate and effect the rapid cycle of technological iteration that characterizes the Web. Aspects of the site are shed as they are rendered obsolete, and new sections resolve. **Ironically,** the site does not contain a lot of the technological bells and whistles that we are known for. The focus has really been on getting people the informa-tion and the tools they need. The site has developed into a real resource for the online design community. The most pleasantly surprising aspect of this is that the community now supports itself. A lot of energy went into setting the site up as a useful resource, but now the visitors help make sure the infor-mation is correct and up-to-date. Tools Computers, Elmer's, plywood, irritants, BBEdit, vi, emacs, Photoshop, GifConverter, Stud Sensor, GifAnimator, digital camera, Wacom tablet, Web Animator, Cosmoworlds, 3 design, Zform, Fetch, Telnet, any means necessary, all browsers, Weblint, nine irons, Eudora, Unix, Mr Snappy

**Cronan Design** 42 Decatur Street, San Francisco, CA 94103 415.522.5800 (dsgn@cronan.com) http://www.cronan.com Since October 1996 Target Design buyers **This site** has a humble set of objectives: a) communicate a basic Web design style; b) provide a visual client list; c) avoid the typical posturing inherent in promotional sites. The site is strictly a visual stimulus, with the exception of an Internet team directory which contains concise bios on team members including staff and outside designers who partner with the studio on various projects. The site is intended to be used in Web capability presentations as distant preliminary review by potential clients. Tools Photoshop, Illustrator, DeBabelizer, Frontpage

**The Designory/Pinkhaus** 211 East Ocean Boulevard, Suite 100, Long Beach, CA 90802 562.432.5707 (dalin.clark@designory.com) http://www.designory.com http://www.pinkhaus.com Since January 1997 Target Anybody with an interest in us or in graphic design Traffic 7500 pages/1700 user sessions per month Awards Eye Candy **The site** is a show-and-tell about our firm, the work we do, and the people who do it. But we wanted to bring something of value to the Web community, not just blow our own horn. In other words, we had to practice what we constantly preach to our clients. We decided to use the site to discuss design issues we feel strongly about, too express our point of view and give others the opportunity to express theirs. We wanted to get visitors to think about design. **We also** chose to use the site as a lab of sorts. To try different, and sometimes less obvious navigation techniques. The first few pages of the site are quite linear, offering users only one path and a somewhat obscure one at that. There are no obvious buttons in the site, except in the discussion area. All navigation is through 'hot' words. The Portfolio section uses an unusual icon-based navigation that we have found very effective. The layered look of the site's opening pages required the use of large photographic images in the background, composited with large type. It took quite a bit of experimenting to achieve an effect we liked that wouldn't take forever to load. Tools Macintosh; Photoshop, Premiere, DeBabelizer, QuarkXpress, SoundEdit, ScreenReady Porsche http://www.porsche.com Since April 1996 Target

60_
61_
62_

50_
51_

80_
81_
82_
142_
143_
144_
145_
146_
147_

Enthusiasts, potential buyers, current owners and the press; in roughly that order Traffic 900,000 pages per month Awards Communication Arts Online Exhibit, EyeCandy, High Five, International Automotive Advertising Awards, Interactive Media and websites; IPPA Award for Design Excellence, DX, Los Angeles Advertising Women, LULU Awards, Interactive Communications The site is unusual for an auto manufacturer in that it gives at least as much weight to brand history and philosophy as it does to providing product information. There is no attempt to overtly drive sales or even increase showroom traffic. Technically and structurally, we have always focused on fairly subtle elements in the site. It is, for instance, mysteriously fast given the size and quality of the images utilized. When the site was launched, the 'bread-crumb' navigation was a new, unique approach to GUI, always giving the user a sense of location in the site structure. This concept has since been widely imitated. The site index was also fairly unique at the time, using the photo icons from the GUI to represent every page on the site in a navigable visual matrix. We have chosen to largely avoid technologies such as Shockwave which can limit potential audience, and slow user exploration. Tools Macintosh, Photoshop, Premiere, QuarkXpress, SoundEdit, ScreenReady and DeBabelizer

**Duffy Design** 901 Marquette Avenue South, Suite 3000, Minneapolis, MN 55402 612.321.2333 152_
(colleen.olson@qm.fallon) http://www.duffy.com Ralston Purina http://www.tidycat.com Since 153_
December 16, 1996 Since its launch in December 1996, the Tidy Cat Web Site (www.tidycat.com) 154_
has revolutionized the cat box filler category's presence on the Internet. By creating a following 155_
among consumers on the Web. Target Cat Owners who are especially interested in the happiness of their cat, and cleanliness of ther home. Awards I.D. Interactive, One Show Silver, British Design and Art Direction Silver, Communications Arts, Art Directors Club of New York Tools Macintosh, Photoshop, Illustrator, BBEdit

**e13** 432 East 13th Street, Apt. 35, New York, NY 10009 212.228.0304 (e13@e13.com) http://www.e13.com 178_
Since January 1997 Target Anyone who wants to see something different Traffic 2,000 hits per 179_
day The style of e13 is derived from a kind of anti-Web design. I've been working as a Web designer for the last several years, and I'm so sick and tired of designing sites for clients with that really lame clean/corporate style that just about every other site uses. I figure since e13 is mine and I know how to use all the latest technology, I can do whatever I want. If I want it to be crazy and ugly, than it's up to me. I'm not worried about losing any sponsors, because I don't want any: this site is completely independent and free-spirited. I think if I ever put an ad on e13, it would destroy everything I've been trying to accomplish. Tools Power Mac, Photoshop, Illustrator, Premiere, BBEdit, Director and lots of screen grabs

**Entropy8** 114 East First Street, Suite 20, New York, NY 10009 USA (chaos@entropy8.com) 54_
http://www.entropy8.com Since June 1996 Target Artists and designers with an eye for the more 55_
conceptual side of the Web Traffic 9,000 visitors per month Awards ID Interactive Media 56_
Review 1997, New York Foundation for the Arts Fellowship, Webby Award, IPPA Award for Design 57_
Excellence Entropy8 began as a way to explore my own objectives with Web design and using the medium to express and evoke response. At the time it was built, few were attempting anything creative or personal and few were doing this well. Business had rushed to get online but the issues of designing for the Web or creation for the Web hadn't been explored. I try to engage the viewer in my visual system from the very start. The navigation bar allows me to create the browser window as a space. The idea of creating a physical feeling of space within the window was important. The content is whatever I happen to be interested in at the moment. Entropy8 is truly my place to experiment. It becomes unusual because I combine technology with the artistry, using technological tricks in artful ways. Tools Macintosh, Photoshop, Illustrator, Premiere and After Effects, BBEdit, Fractal Painter and Detailer, GifBuilder, Studio Pro

**Evolve Design** 914 North Curson Avenue, West Hollywood, CA 90046 213.876.9498 (evolvedesign@ 63_
evolvedesign.com) http://www.evolvedesign.com Since May 1996 Target Graphic design studios and designers, and clients for freelance print and Web design work The site is designed to have a minimalist, modern look, without getting bogged down with too much wild cybernetic type and graphics. I like using layers of imagery and type to convey a sense of depth in the printed pieces I design. I wanted to portray the same sense of style in my website, however, I didn't want to use 3-D

forms and type to achieve it literally. The bright red menu buttons pop against the white background, placing the menu plane in front of the main viewing window. Type running over background images also re-enforces the depth of the pages. I have a sense of humor and a technical educational background, and I wanted to convey these aspects of my personality, both of which influence my design. Thus, the numerous scientific references and icons, as well as the sometimes hokey graphics. **Tools** Photoshop, Illustrator, Pagemill, GIFBuilder

**Ken Feingold** 140 Fifth Avenue, New York, NY 10011 212.645.9485 (kenf@panix.com) 174_
http://www2.sva.edu/ken Since December 1994 **Target** People interested in visual art **Awards** DNP 175_ Awards 1996 Interactive Award **The site** is part of ongoing experimentation in my work, what Erkki Huhtamo in his artintact3 essay has referred to as 'meta-interactivity.' There are a number of 'hidden' links which change from time-to-time **Tools** Perl, C, Photoshop, GifBuilder, BBEdit, Director, Shockwave, SoundEdit16, various SGI image-processing tools

**FontNet** 65-69 East Road, London N1 6AH UK +44 (0)171.490.5390 (barrd@type.co.uk) 52_ http://www.type.co.uk Since December 1995 **Target** Ad agencies, designers, typographers, anyone 53_ interested in type **Traffic** 6,000 hits per day **The site** represents a simple approach to the age-old problem of navigation. Neville Brody developed a visual molecular system that guides the viewer through a large site with multiple layers. Kept clean and simple to avoid the plethora of plugins available on the Net, which makes the intended job of information gathering impossible. Feedback on the whole from our visitors has been positive. Our formula for success stems from Maximum Impact Minimum Memory (MISM) in which we believe that with a little extra effort download times can be kept to a minimum **Tools** Power Macintosh, Photoshop, Freehand, BBEdit, Silicon Graphics server

**Giant Step** 820 West Jackson, Suite 400, Chicago, IL 60605 312.470.2700 (eric@giantstep.com) 36_ http://www.giantstep.com Since November 1995 **Target** New business opportunities and the 37_ press **Awards** ID Magazine Interactive Design Award **The site** is being generated dynamically from 38_ a database using active server pages. We are also doing browser detection and offering a bit 39_ of a different site to those using Internet Explorer. **Tools** Photoshop, Illustrator, MS InterDev Studio, Director, SQL

**John Hersey Illustration** 546 Magnolia Avenue, Larkspur, CA 94939 415.927.2091 (ultraduc@hersey.com) 23_ http://www.hersey.com Since August 1996 **Target** Clients of course, but visitors are mainly art 24_ students around the world **Traffic** 1000-2000 hits per day **The way** my site looks derives from how I like 25_ things to look. It's very organic and natural to my way of thinking. It has no grid and tends to be very changeable. **Tools** Photoshop, QuickTime VR, GifBuilder

**IBM Corporate Internet Programs** 55 Broad Street, New York, NY 10004 212.612.1915 (webmaster@ 137_ www.ibm.com) http://www.ibm.com Since May 1994 **Target** Current and potential IBM customers, 138_ shareholders, business partners, press, consultants/analysts, consumers **Traffic** 700,000 visitors/week 139_ **Awards** AIGA Graphic Design USA, CASIA Award **Given IBM's** panoply of products and services – 140_ the company makes over 50,000 products, does business in over 150 countries, and employs over 200,000 141_ people - our biggest challenge is keeping things simple. We use many of the same tools and solutions and services that IBM sells to our customers; we also work closely with the company's development teams to develop and test new products and technologies. **Tools** Our server runs on a set of RS/6000 SP massively parallel supercomputers hosted by the IBM Global Network. We use Lotus Notes/ Domino for most project management and communication, also Photoshop, Premiere and Fusion

restart

**idealab!** 790 East Colorado Boulevard, Suite 210, Pasadena, CA 91101 818.244.6897 (idealab@aol.com)        150_
http://www.idealab.com Since September 1996 Target everybody interested in internet commerce        151_
or services Traffic 6,000 hits per day The site had to be well-designed and executed to build credibility
and confidence in the foster companies. The layout of the site is simple and easy to navigate. The
graphic navigation buttons at the bottom of each page allow visitors to move anywhere in the site with a
maximum of two mouse clicks. This simplicity is carried through to each dependent company.
The idealab! site focuses on the two areas that are most important to its success. First, the talents of the
idealab! team. Second, the foster company pages focus attention on each of the offspring and
provide a gateway to that company's Internet presence. The Internet 'front door' of each company is
included to give a taste of the high quality of individual user interface design. Tools Photoshop,
HotMetaL PRO, in-house tools for color palette refinement and common page header/footer merging

**I-D Gruppe** Dewanger Strasse 22, 73457 Essingen, Germany +49.7365.96050 (idgruppe@idgruppe.com)        158_
http://www.idgruppe.com Swatch http://www.swatch.com Since February 1996 Target Swatch        159_
fans Traffic 1 million hits per day Awards 90 awards worldwide The website debuted with an online
press conference for 6,000 journalists, held offline at artist Nam June Paik's New York City
studio. The website's net hunt was one of the largest worldwide online games, with teams from 75
countries fighting to find the mosaic of puzzle pieces hidden on 10 different Internet servers.
In 1996 we created the largest Christmas tree ever, with thousands of decorations from visitors. For
the future, we plan many exciting applications, which will be – in the tradition of Swatch –
a surprise. Tools Photoshop

**Ikonic Inc** 2 Harrison Street, Top Floor, San Francisco, CA 94105 415.908.8000 (acorona@ikonic.com)        116_
http://www.ikonic.com Virgin Records America http://www.virginrecords.com Since August 1996        117_
Awards I.D. Magazine Design Award 1997 Rather than present Virgin as an overly commercialized or
domineering force in music, Ikonic designed the site to show Virgin off as the music fan's label.
This was accomplished by building a site that pushes featured artists to the top of the site by creating
fan sub-sites that, when possible, link to the thousands of fan sites already in existence on the
Web. Virgin also aimed to break new ground in providing entertaining functionality around the music.
Ikonic designed, engineered, and developed several ways to explore audio content on the Web.
The site gives music fans a way to preview whole music tracks, and browse more in-depth information
on a particular artist, while giving Virgin an additional channel for promotion and distribution of
new music. Both RealAudio and Shockwave technology are employed on the site to evoke a musical
experience that is refreshing to media-hungry Web surfers. The homepage design is highly extensible,
allowing Virgin to switch out featured artists frequently through a modular system defined by
four-quadrant typography/photography-based elements. The overall architecture of the site houses
Virgin corporate information, Virgin labels, and individual sub-sites for each of the bands featured
on the home page. These sub-sites have their own home pages, information areas, features, functionality
and art direction. The corporate and Virgin label look draws from existing Virgin collateral and
label campaigns bringing them to the next level of on-line design. Tools Macintosh 7600/132, Dell
P133, Real Audio, Photoshop, Illustrator, DeBabelizer, Director, Deck II, SoundEdit

**i/o 360 digital design inc** 841 Broadway, Suite 502, New York, NY 10003 212.533.4467 (gong@io360.com)        17_
http://www.io360.com Since June 1996 Target Design aficionados, Web weirdos Traffic 2000        19_
per day i/o 360's design philosophy is based on the premise that visual computing has and will continue        20_
to profoundly affect the way we communicate. With the advent of graphical user interfaces,        21_
multimedia, distributed networks, real-time 3D graphics engines, and a rich set of design and devel-        22_
opment tools and programming languages, the role of the visual designer requires one to be a        156_
strategist, communicator, marketer, identity-maker, applications developer, and interaction designer.        157_
The convergence of broadcast, print, radio, and computational media translates into immense
opportunities for businesses worldwide, and the vehicle is the flux and change in today's rapidly evolving
information and communications technologies. To be a digital designer in today's marketplace
is to embrace the ever-shifting forces that shape the development of technology and the economics
which support them. i/o 360's ongoing mission is to be positioned at the nexus where visual

design, logical function, and the demanding complexity of technology converge. The website is divided
in two halves: 'OY' Client Work, and 'YO' Experiments and Outtakes. The website design itself is
engineered to degrade to lower-end browsers, but utilizes JAVA, GIF animation, and Macromedia's
Shockwave Plug-in. The black-and-white grid motif was designed to create a structured and
modular 'field', upon which illustrations of our work and their descriptions would hang as foreground
elements. Each individual section of the website is a subtle variation on this grid, the layout of
internal elements being manipulated like musical notes on a staff. The site was developed and managed
by Mksite 2.1, an i/o 360-developed website development tool which runs in the UNIX environment. Tools i/o 360 Mksite 2.1, Photoshop, Illustrator, Director, Emacs, VI, Kinetix 3D Studio MAX 1.2,
Pagemill, NetObjects Fusion, After Effects, Symantec Cafe, Microsoft Visual J++, GifBuilder,
Premiere, FutureSplash Animator Sotheby's http://www.sothebys.com Since August 1995 Target
New collectors Awards Art Director's Club New York, CASIE The website was produced in
the early years of the Web, back when HTML 1.0 was considered radical. We opted to push the static
nature of the Web 'page' metaphor to the max, and used a lot of white space to foreground more
typographic and abstract treatments in Sothebys' goal to establish a Web presence with a decidedly
younger audience. Tools Photoshop, After Effects, BBEdit, MKSITE 1.0, Perl

Jodi F.Halstraat 61, Lisse 2162CL Netherlands (jodi@jodi.org) http://www.jodi.org Since August 1995     170_
<< Hi, The URL you submitted was not added to Yahoo because we feel that there is currently not     171_
enough interesting content within your site for our users. When your site is more fully developed, please     172_
resubmit your listing. We believe that this policy is the best for all parties involved. Users are quickly     173_
turned off by underdeveloped sites. It reflects poorly not only on the site itself, but [on] Yahoo as well.
We look forward to adding your site once the underlying content is more fully developed. Thanks,
The Yahoo Gang >>

Eto Kouichirou 2-12-21 Imagawa Suginami, Tokyo, 167 Japan (eto@sfc.keio.ac.jp) http://andro.sfc.     32_
keio.ac.jp/eto Since December 1993 Target Virtual space researchers Traffic Quality of traffic,     33_
not quantity is what's important My Web page design is based on my concept of 'moving.' I especially     34_
think the effect is important; not just a moving part of the page but the whole moving page.     35_
When you enter my site, you will see the fade-in effect with the color of the page changing from
white to black. When the whole page is displayed you can only see the word 'eto.' I believe this
effect makes the whole display shine. Right now I'm not using Java or Shockwave positively because
I do not see any advantage in Java for designing the Web page. It is a good tool for changing the
platform of communications like Marimba, but not a tool for making animation. So I use these technologies as a way of changing the structure of communications. Tools Emacs, perl, netpbm,
Photoshop

LettError Type & Typography c/o Laan van Meerdervoort 1f, NL 2517AA Den Haag, Netherlands     44_
+31.70.3605025 (evb@knoware.nl) http://www.letterror.com Since 1995 Target Designers, programmers,     45_
people interested in type & typography on and off the Web Traffic 600 hits per day Awards The
LettError Award for Most Patient website We designed and built our own database-based Web authoring
machine because there were no satisfying tools we could find. Databases contain every scrap
of data concerning the site; not only content, images, text etc. but also the layout of various pages and
structures. The site is compiled with a program written in Python that takes the databases and
resolves all references, links, images etc. The site can be maintained without writing any HTML. Tools
Macintosh, FileMaker Pro, Python, LettError custom site compiler, SiteRipper, Fetch, Netscape,
BBEdit FontFontFinder http://www.fontfont.de Since Summer 1996 Target Designers, people looking
for fonts Traffic 5000 hits per day Awards The LettError Award for Most Automated website.
The FontFont library consists of about 1000 fonts by roughly 80 designers. Production of this website

stop

had to be automated as much as possible: it would by unpractical to maintain about 3000 pages
by hand. FontShop already maintained a set of databases about their fonts; ID numbers, names, catalog
numbers, styles, etc. Those databases became the basis of the website. By cross-referencing
the data a lot of inconsistencies were found and dealt with. Then the databases were extended to contain
more site specific information: whether images had been generated, how the packages were
formed. **A special** tool was written using SmallTalk Agents that takes the databases and generates all
the necessary pages, including indexes of designers, fonts and packages, etc. A secondary system,
the LettError SiteRipper, was used to make all additional pages in the database that did not fit
in the font databases. All the font specimen images were generated with software written in Python.
Again taking the databases, but adding specimen specific information, the program would take
a CD-ROM full of fonts and turn it into a mass of images. The imaging system takes all these considerations into account. Updating the site now consists of updating the databases (which has to
happen anyway) exporting the data, and generating the pages and the extra images. **Tools** Python (with
various custom applications for development and maintenance), SmallTalk Agents, SmallTalk
(custom application), FileMaker Pro, PhotoShop, Illustrator, GifBuilder

**M.A.D.** PO Box 190, Sausalito, CA 94965 415.331.1023 (mad@madxs.com) **http://www.madxs.com**          4_
**Since** Summer 1995 **Target** Ad agencies, corporate creative services, design and illustration buyers          6_
**Awards** AIGA **The site** predates tables, frames, and other more sophisticated layout tools. M.A.D. wanted          74_
to see if it was possible to create a compelling site given this primitive state of Web software          75_
development. Our challenge was to demonstrate that a clean use of typography, a white background,          76_
and simple icons could be more powerful and interesting than tacky color backgrounds and 3-D          77_
buttons. Our principle innovations were first, to program a 'code' tag to our text so that the screen font
was always Courier, regardless of the font viewers designated on their browsers, and second,
to utilize a system of 'blanks' – transparent Gif spacers – to control the placement of text and images
so that the browser window was a complete composition, not just another receptacle for more
flotsam and jetsam. **Tools** Photoshop, Illustrator, Director, Netscape, HTML editor, Webmap, Quicktime
**Funnel http://www.funnel.com Since** March 1996 **Target** The curious and brave **Awards** DNP
(Japan), AIGA, San Francisco Museum of Modern Art Permanent Collection **M.A.D.'s intention** is to disrupt
lowest-common denominator notions of how this new medium should look and work. To achieve
this we used the Shockwave plug-in to animate sequences that blend with background images to fill up
the entire screen. The opening sequence has a funnel the viewer can draw with.In the Misinfor-
mation section, the type needs to be physically pulled with the cursor in order to be read. **Tools** Photoshop,
Illustrator, Premiere, Director and Shockwave, Netscape, Simple Text, Sound Edit, RayDream3d

**MetaDesign** 350 Pacific Avenue, 3rd Floor, San Francisco, CA 94111 415.627.0790 (info@metadesign.com)          70_
**http://www.metadesign.com Since** March 1996 **Target** Potential clients and potential employees,          71_
the design industry, and the general public **Traffic** 5,000 hits/week **Awards** AIGA – Design of Under-          72_
standing 2, How Magazine – 1996 Self-Promotion Award and International Design Competition          73_
Merit, NetGuide Live – Best of the Web, Print – 1996 Digital Design Award **In today's** globally-wired
markets – where interested parties are not necessarily always nearby – a multicultural perspective
and exchange of skills and ideas across geographical boundaries can only enhance a firm's offer.
The problem, therefore, was to create a website for a multidisciplinary design firm, which, with
offices in San Francisco, Berlin, and London, needs to present a common and unified face despite
its diverse locations. The site is, therefore, a concise representation of who MetaDesign is and
what we can offer: savvy solutions that function down to detail level, where every detail is a part of a
larger whole. **With such** an emphasis on detail work, the biggest – and probably most common –
problem was displaying archived project work that would show those details but load efficiently. Initial
studies showed that large multiple images at an early hierarchical level of the site would be a
problem in this regard. The site was then reorganized to include a whole new bottom level (with large
detailed images), exhaustive experiments in image compression and 'bit-stripping' providing
the rest of the solution. **Tools** Photoshop, Illustrator, BBEdit, DeBabelizer, GifBuilder, Netscape
Enterprise Server, SimpleText

**Moscow Media** 11 East 32nd Street, Suite 7E, New York, NY 10016 212.447.0115 (editor@moscowchan-
nel.com) **http://www.moscowchannel.com** Since July 1996 **Target** Everyone **Traffic** Anywhere
from 150,000-500,000 hits per month. **Awards** Magellan 4 Star Site, USA Today Hot Site, The Net
Magazine Site of the Month, NetGuide Gold Site, Yahoo Pick of the Week, Microsoft Explorer
Start Page Best of the Net, Mecklermedia IWORLD Site of the Day, Microsoft Network UK Site of
the Day, The Village Voice Best of the Net, The Russian America Award, Awesome Universal
Top 500 Best of the Net. **While most** sites target the Internet mainstream – young people living in
the U.S., probably using the latest browsers – Moscow Channel is meant to be appreciated by
netizens all over the world possessing various degrees of technical proficiency and software. Feedback
and traffic statistics reflects this diversity. **Visually,** Moscow Channel was designed with the goal
of accentuating the site's content and making it easy to access and navigate. On the interface level,
the frames-based layout enables the reader to view and access the journal's entire content from
each of its pages. In terms of layout, the individual pages have been kept relatively spare and uncrowded;
the emphasis has been kept on making the process of digesting the page as easy as possible.
**Moscow Channel** is edited and designed with the goal of facilitating in-depth reading and viewing.
Judging by our server's statistics, these efforts have paid off. Allowing our visitors to view outside
links while remaining within the site's framework is another way in which we try to make the experience
of visiting Moscow Channel a little more stable – more conducive to thinking than surfing.
**Tools** Macintosh; Photoshop, Pagemill, DeBabelizer, GIFBuilder, Word, Netscape Navigator

108_
109_

**Nike** One Bowerman Drive, Beaverton, OR 97005 503.671.6453 (matthew.childs@nike.com)
**Title IX http://www.nike.com** Since June 23, 1997 **Title IX** is a splash to the nike.com site and the
first screen you'd come to when logging into www.nike.com. It was launched on June 23, the
25th anniversary of the signing of Title IX, which states: "No person in the United States shall, on the
basis of sex, be excluded from participation in, be denied the benefits of, or be subjected to
discrimination under any education program or activiity receiving Federal financial assistance – June
23, 1972." **Through** the juxtaposition of outdated quotes and modern-day achievements by
women we were able to illustrate the advancement of women in sports. This was a perfect piece for
Nike to do since it illustrates their commitment to all athletes and to sport.

127_
129_
130_
131_
132_
133_
134_
135_

**Post Tool Design** 301 Eighth Street, San Francisco, CA 94103 415.255.1094 (david@posttool.com)
**www.posttool.com Post Tv http://www.posttv.com** Since August 1996 **Target** We are trying
to reach people with a sense of humor **Traffic** 2000-5500 hits per day **Post Tv** is to the Web what
The Honeymooners, Johnny Carson, Dinah Shore, I Love Lucy and the rest were to television.
Really. The site appears simple, but is in fact one of the only sources of 'coordinated' sound streaming and animation on the Web. As technology such as Marimba becomes more widely used, we
will incorporate background downloading to send weekly 'updates' to each section of our site. **Tools**
Photoshop, Illustrator, Director, Infini-d

30_ †∨
31_

**Postmasters** 80 Greene Street, New York NY 10012 212.941.5711 (postmasters@thing,net)
**http//:thing.net/~pomaga** Since March 1996 **Target** denizens of the art world **The website** was designed
to play off recognition and 'misrecognition' on the part of viewers. The expected navigation
controls are masked so that they appear like components taken from a binary calculator. Many people
familiar with conventions of the Web probably have some experience with a calculator, or at
least the symbolic notation for such operations as addition, subtraction, and division. By placing these
symbols where Web interfaces often display navigation controls, we tried to create a condition for
participants so they can enjoy a kind of game where they can match or map two different things they
know about, but which they probably never thought about as related or superimposed. The list

180_
181_
182_
183_
184_
185_

of binary numerals is composed of only two images: one for the numeral 1 and one for the 0. They are composed in HTML to produce all the numbers seen, each of which stands for one of the artists in the exhibit and thus, functions as a randomly accessible directory into the website. We wanted to give both a random way of accessing the site as well as a linear one, for which we give the navigation controls on each page.

**Powazek Productions** 660 Third Street, San Francisco, CA 94107 415.865.0720 (derek@powazek.com) 110_ http://www.powazek.com The fray http://www.fray.com Since September 1996 Target Anyone 111_ with a story to tell Traffic 10,000 pages a day on average Awards Cool Site of the Day, Project Cool Sighting, MSN Pick of the Day, USA Today Hot Site of the Day Instead of fighting against the current of the Web, designers should go with what it does best – they should work within the medium. That means being clever, not extravagant. Good design on the Web does not mean giant JPEG graphics, beautiful as they may be. It means smart design, for the medium. Designing for the Web is the opposite of designing for print. Print designers get used to controlling every last bit, every last line, every last ligature. But design for the Web means understanding that every computer will render your pages a little differently – different fonts, different resolutions, different browsers. Good Web design is about graceful degradation: making sure your pages work in any browser, whether it supports the latest whiz-bang extension or not. Tools Macintosh, Photoshop, BBEdit, DeBabelizer

**Razorfish Inc** 107 Grand Street, 3rd Floor, New York, NY 10013 212.966.5960 (kanarick@razorfish.com) 64_ http://www.razorfish.com Since January 1995 Target Tastemakers in the online world, decision- 65_ makers at Fortune 500 companies and their agents, media and entertainment companies, online services, adventurous people, and space aliens. Awards New Visions/New Voices This site is a dynamic demonstration of how we think about the shifting, evanescent intersection of content, technology, marketing, and design. It provides a complex, compelling, and comprehensive experience. Visitors have a choice of four different 'modes,' allowing the user some control over the speed and format of content. Furthermore, the site is dynamically generated based upon user choices, viewing patterns, user software and hardware, and other data. The site includes a number of randomly generated elements and features a 'vibe' window which previews other areas of the site. In the 'XL' version, the site includes proprietary Java software performing a number of unique functions, including an 'activity meter,' a 'depth meter,' and a multimedia presentation system. The site exemplifies the next generation of Internet experiences, transforming how people use and think about the Web. Utilizing original Java applets, the site actively responds to the user. For example, animations in the navigation bar at the top of the page speed up as new pages are downloaded, then slow down again when they have finished. Likewise, when users are inactive the frames will change on their own, animating a series of colorful details taken from elsewhere within the site. The Razorfish logo, presented in both two and three dimensions on the site, is composed of three overlapping gear-like elements that reflect the many interlocking facets of the company. Tools Photoshop, Illustrator, Acrobat, Fetch, DeBabelizer, GifBuilder, Symantec Cafe, GifWizard, Visual C++, Front Page, Word, Excel, Telnet, Internet Explorer, Netscape Navigator, Strata 3-D, Caligari TrueSpace, Microsoft Outlook, Vignette Story Server, The Palace, RealAudio, After Effects, Premiere, Avid VideoShop, SimpleText, Radius Edit, SoundEdit, Director

**R/GA Digital Studios** 350 West 39th Street, New York, NY 10018 212.946.4000 (e-mail web@rga.com) 46_ http://www.rga.com Since December 1996 Traffic approximately 900 distinct hosts per month 47_ The site is an expression of a group of ideas that guide our interactive work. Many of these grow 48_ out of our experience in digital game design. We believe engaging and immersive experiences 49_ can be built out of simple rule systems. We also try to build visual and narrative complexity using small, easily recombinable elements. Finally, we try to structure interaction so that users are themselves 'designers.' At the same time the site addresses specific company goals. As a design firm we are, of course, in the business of selling our services, and want to reach potential clients. This site is a valuable part of a dialogue with these people on just what interactive design is, and what we might be able to provide. The company has a 20-year reputation for excellence in visual design. Here we are able to demonstrate this in a way that underscores the technical and logical rigor behind the beautiful images. The site called for a combination of technically challenging elements, including the fixed grid design, animation involving large portions of the screen, and on-the-fly assembly through a backend database. Early on, we settled on Java as the best way to realize our

conception, but this choice was not without negative consequences. We are still very excited
by the promise of this technology, but did grow frustrated with it in the short term. Implementation
from browser to browser proved to be rather 'un-universal' and we are still hearing from
potential viewers who can't see our site through their firewall. Tools Programmed mainly in Java,
also Photoshop and HTML

**Salon Internet** 185 Berry Street, Suite 4811, San Francisco, CA 94107 415.977.1999 (salon@salon
1999.com) Salon http://www.salonmagazine.com Since November 1995 Target People who
like to read, who appreciate insightful commentary and irreverent prose Traffic 2.6 million page views
per month Awards Cool Web Designers of the Year; Print, Society of Publication Designers,
Graphis; Time's Best Web Site of the Year, Ad Age Online Magazine of the Year, Web Magazine Webby
Our content is original to our site, and we strive to differentiate ourselves by this fact, by the
fact that we update it five days a week and, more importantly, by the varied mix we present through
the unique voice of our editors and writers. We attempt to create a compelling site for people
who love to read and the numbers show that we have succeeded. Our style is, of necessity, spare,
thoughtful and elegant, well suited to the Web with its varying modes of delivery. We often use
illustration and work closely with our artists to ensure manageable file sizes while maintaining the
integrity of the artist's style and ideas. All the designers have a thorough knowledge of HTML
and are responsible for keeping abreast of changes in software and HTML standards. Tools Photoshop,
Illustrator, BBEdit, DeBabelizer, Netscape, Internet Explorer, QuickTime, SoundEdit Pro and
an assortment of Web-specific software

112_
113_
114_
115_

**Second Story** (formerly Brad Johnson Presents) 239 NW 13th Avenue, Suite 215, Portland, OR 97209
503.827.7155 (bradj@secondstory.com) http://www.secondstory.com National Geographic Online
http://www.nationalgeographic.com The River Wild Running the Selway Since June 1996 Target Anyone
interested in travel, river rafting or wildlife watching Awards 1997 How International Design
Annual Merit Award, High Five Award, CNET Best of the Web. This site was our first implementation
of an architectural model that has become central to our navigation philosophy: to balance a
narrative quality with random accessibility. In this way, users are 'led' through the site by means of a
narrative journal, but have at the same time the ability to access any of the resources at will.
Tools Photoshop, Illustrator, Web Weaver Dinosaur Eggs Since August 1996 Target All ages. Awards
Communication Arts Design Annual, Yahoo Pick of the Week, IPPA Design Ace Award, Coolest
on the Web (Science Category), Project Cool Tools Photoshop, Illustrator, Web Weaver, Elastic Reality
The Fantastic Forest Since November 1996 Target Students Awards High Five Award, Cool
Sighting, Project Cool, Macromedia Shocked Site of the Week This website utilizes many of the features
of Netscape Navigator 3.0. The 'borderless' frames create a seamless CD-ROM-like multimedia
experience. The site has QuickTime sound, QuickTime VR panoramas, Shockwave, Javascript cookies
and a CGI custom certificate generator. The site takes the form of a map and a set of sites to
visit along the map's trail. Each forest element was created as a separate watercolor, then patched
together with HTML and JavaScript. Sounds enhance the trip every step of the way. Tools
Photoshop, Illustrator, Web Weaver, Strata Studio Pro, SoundEdit 16 Kaikoura Expedition Since February
1997 Target Anyone interested in travel, natural history or science Awards Yahoo Pick of the
Week This site was built from scratch in a foreign country in three days. It is the first known 'live
event' site that was designed and built in the field. For more than two weeks, dispatches were
sent every business day that included QuickTime video clips, original 3-D interactive illustrations, QTVRs,
sounds and photography. Tools Photoshop, Premiere, AfterEffects, Illustrator, Web Weaver,
BBEdit, Studio Pro

94_
95_
96_
97_
98_
99_
100_
101_

**ShaG** 715B Clementina Street, San Francisco, CA 94103 415.255.4544 (shag@sirius.com)     93_
http://www.sirius.com/~shag Since February 1996 Target Anyone with a computer and modem
Traffic 5,000 hits per month Awards Eye Candy The Web at its best is a free information/disinfor-
mation entertainment medium. So that's what we feed back to it. The site is essentially a self-promotion,
but with no links to our commercial work. We like to make stuff that's fun for us, and presumably,
the outside world. Even the most schizophrenic (dis)organization suggests a sense of order on some
level. There is no official format or style as long as it's viewable online and we like it. A fair
percentage of our 400 pages rely on bold pixel-y icons to get to the next page, with no real descrip-
tion of what's next. It's okay to drop text out of the whole thing, too, because some of the surfers
might not be old enough to read or are from a land that doesn't use English. We don't tell
people that they are going to need plugins to view our site or what browser you're supposed to have,
etc, no warnings. Sorry if you crashed again. Tools Any shareware available online; we'll use
anything we can get our hands on. We might use something brand-new once, then never touch it
again. Real workhorses: SimpleText, Netscape, GifBuilder, Shockwave, QuickTime

**Speak Magazine** 301 Eighth Street, Suite 240, San Francisco, CA 94103 415.431.5396 (publish     102_
@speakmag.com) http://www.speakmag.com Since Spring 1996 Target 18-29 year old market     103_
Traffic To tell the truth, we never thought the site was all that special. The printed magazine has always     104_
come first. When we think of the site, we choose elements from the magazine that would be     105_
interesting in motion, and then we have fun with the sequencing. We like to preserve mystery by offering
pieces to a larger puzzle (that hopefully will be solved by buying or subscribing to the magazine).
Because content is less critical in our site, we can just enjoy the dynamics of the elements and play with
the rhythm of discovery that is intrinsic to Web navigation. The print elements are almost never
computer-generated. We usually use photos and drawings, with very little Photoshop manipulation or
computer-looking stuff. We like to keep the natural humanity in the objects and forms we choose.
Tools Photoshop, Illustrator, QuarkXPRess, paper-copier machines, ink, pencils, paper, 35mm camera,
scanner, hands and feet

**Studio Grafico Theo van Boxel** Lungarno Galileo Galilei 14 56125 Pisa – Italy + 39.50.28381     26_
(thebox@cibernet.it) http://www.cybernet.it/thebox Since February 1996 Target everyone interested     27_
in good design Traffic approximately 600 per week Tools Illustrator, Photoshop, BBEdit, DeBabelizer,     28_
GifBuilder, Director     29_

**Thirst** 117 South Cook, Suite 333, Barrington, IL 60010 847.842.0222 (Thirstype@aol.com)     160_
Fisher Bicycle http://www.fisherbikes.com Since April 1997 Target Bike-riders, non-bike-riders, and all
others Traffic 6000 sessions 156,000 hits per week The aim is to delight, inform, and entertain, all
with the minimum of fuss. Gary Fisher bicycles are technically amazing machines; the aim of the engineering is to provide a thrilling and enjoyable biking experience. The bikes are solidly-built but light-weight,
and are recognized for their unique 'feel.' We hope that the same may be said for the website. Our biggest
technical hurdle was controlling the uncontrollable. Our advice? Marry content to context. Remember
that the screen is not paper. Do not waste anybody's time or energy. Make every graphic and word count
for something, and lead somewhere. Avoid the obvious tricks. Keep the bandwidth as skinny as
possible. Tools Fontographer, QuarkXPress, Photoshop, BBEdit, proprietary software

**UCSB, Department of Art Studio, Electronic Art & Theory (EAT) Lab** Santa Barbara, CA 93105     188_
805.893.8448 (vesna@arts.ucsb.edu) http://www.arts.ucsb.edu/bodiesinc A tongue-in-cheek     189_
commentary on some of the more obvious contradictions of corporate culture, particularly for     190_
those working with art and technology, Bodies INCorporated addresses such issues as the legitimacy     191_
of cultural institutions as the only socially sanctioned site for display of art, and the ways in
which structures of physical and ephemeral spaces effect our collectively embodied behavior. It is
a collaborative project on many levels, from the team of artists implementing it, to the actively
participating audience attempting to gain shares in the body of work. The main elements of the online
site are three constructed environments: Limbo Incorporated, where information about inert
bodies that have been put on hold – bodies whose owners have abandoned or neglected them –

is accessed; Necropolis Incorporated, where owners can either look at or choose how they wish their bodies to die; and Showplace Incorporated, where members can participate in discussion forums, view star/featured bodies of the week, bet in the 'deadpools', and enter 'dead' or 'alive' chat sessions. **Tools** 3-D models from Viewpoint Data Labs, Alias/Wavefront, Cosmo Create, Photoshop, Infini-D, Premiere, SoundEdit 16, RealAudio, Java, JavaScript, CGI/Perl, PioneerPro, CosmoWorld, Live3d, CosmoPlayer

**Waters Design Associates Inc** 3 West 18th Street, New York, NY 10011 212.807.0717 (michelle@waters design.com) http://www.watersdesign.com Second Harvest http://www.secondharvest.org **Since** August 1996 **Target** The purpose of the site is to increase awareness and encourage support for hunger-relief efforts among individuals, communities and corporations. Targeted to many levels of interest, the site includes searching capabilities and information for member food banks, legal and financial disclosures for the media and watchdog organizations, and an online newsletter and events calendar for the curious browser. **Traffic** 1,500 to 2,000 hits per month. **Awards** USA Today Hot Site of the Day, Cool Central Cool Site Award, Association of Graphic Communication Special Merit Award **The interface** of the site was designed to be direct and intuitive. A dramatic welcome screen introduces the mission of the organization to guests. The site is centered on a comprehensive site map, following the welcome screen, that contains an overview of the content and serves to orient the viewer. To ease navigation further, every page of the site contains a similar set of navigation buttons in a fixed location. **Waters Design** Associates designed and programmed the initial site and provided additional design services for the first six months of operation. The firm also provided training services for the Second Harvest staff, allowing the organization to update and maintain the site in-house. The simplicity, yet great depth, of the Second Harvest site allows for frequent updates and exploits the true potential of the World Wide Web – timely and direct communication. **Tools** GNN Press, BBEdit, GIF Converter, Photoshop, HTML and CGI Programming

124_
125_
126_

**Wired Digital** 660 Third Street, San Francisco, CA 94107 415.276.8412 (barbara@wired.com) http://www.hotwired.com **Since** October 1994 **Target** Web-savvy professionals **Traffic** more than 600,000 members **Awards** ID Magazine Interactive Media; Best Web Site, Time Magazine; Still Cool Site of the Year, Internet Community Awards; Best Web Site of the Year, Digital Hollywood Awards; Best Arts and Entertainment Site, The National Infrastructure Award **HotWired** has consistently tried to push the edge of HTML and Web development. We have also tried to break from the traditions of other media (print, broadcast) in developing content specifically for the Web, while maintaining design, editorial, and production sensibilities that are typically Wired. This has been manifested in everything from our constant evaluation of bleeding-edge technology to our participation in Web standards bodies, fighting for advances in design capabilities in Web-based languages. **One of** our biggest challenges is conveying our aesthetic in a medium with such fierce bandwidth limitations. We've struggled over the years, constantly anticipating a breakthrough in modem technologies, only to be disappointed as the Web advanced and speed did not. We've refined and evolved our design axioms of simplicity, clarity, and boldness as a result. Originally, HotWired was designed to be low-res, with a hand-made look to signify humans talking to humans, not machines interfacing with machines. As bandwidth (transmission time) increases, so does resolution, but it still is important to have a simple, clear, and direct design approach, and to avoid a cold, shiny, computer look. **We're** also beginning to experiment with full-scale push-media publishing. We've been exploring the new dynamic HTML technologies, as well as other interactive ways of communicating and building relationships with our audience. **Tools** Macintosh, with generic PC clones for cross-platform testing. Web servers: SGI and Sun UltraSparcs. Photoshop, Illustrator, BBEdit, Debabelizer and GIFBuilder; most automated production tools written in-house; servers run Apache

13_
83_
85_
86_
87_

Post Tool Design
LettError
Aufuldfish & Warinner
Terbo Ted
Robert Appleton

**Zimmermann Crowe Design** 90 Tehama Street, San Francisco, CA 94105 415.777.5560 (dennis@ 78_
zcd.com) http://www.zcd.com Since March 1997 Target Design- and technology-savvy clients 79_
with backbones. The site is aimed at potential clients with ISDN-or-faster connections so we weren't
as concerned with super-small file sizes, opting for higher-quality images instead The website
features an opening animation and downloadable QuickTime movies in a portfolio of our diverse capabilities, and also hopefully conveys some of the enthusiasm for design that permeates our work.
We hope to attract clients with a similar enthusiasm. Since we're graphic designers, and very picky about
type and imagery, we went for total control by not having any HTML text in the site. All the copy
was imbedded in graphics. We wanted to control the typeface, the size, the rag Tools QuarkXPress,
Photoshop, Illustrator, Premiere, Agfa Arcus II scanner

**Zupergraphyx!** Napoleon Annicqstraat 51 B-9600 Ronse Belgium 32.55.20.88.63 (msamyn@innet.be) 166_
http://www.riv.be/Zuper/signature Group Z http://www.adaweb.com/~GroupZ Since November
1995 Target Online art enthusiasts, people who like to be entertained on the Web, technical sado-
masochists This is not a virtual art gallery. The works on the Group Z site exist nowhere else.
All works try to go as far as possible technically and artistically with the limited means of Web browsers.
Tools Netscape Navigator, Programmer's File Editor, Photostyler, Director, Cooledit, Music Draw

Graphis Magazine **Graphis** Books

OSTER

Typogr

GRAPHIS LETTERHEAD

LETTERHEAD

WORLD

100

TRADE

YRS

MARKS

WORLD TRADEMARKS

GRAPHIS DIGITAL FONTS

DIGITALFONTS

GRAPHIS STUDENT DESIGN

STUDENTDESIG

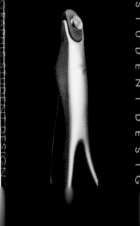

GRAPHIS NEW MEDIA 1

IMAGE COLLECTION
JUST CLICK TO PREVIEW

NEW MEDIA 1

RICHARD SAUL WURMAN

# INFORMATION
# ARCHITECTS

In·for·ma·tion Ar·chi·tect [L *info-
tectus*] n. 1) the individual who
organizes the patterns inherent
in data, *making the complex
clear.* 2) a person who creates
the structure or map of information which allows others to
find their personal paths to
knowledge. 3) the emerging 21st
century professional occupation
addressing the needs of the age
focused upon clarity, human understanding and the science of
the organization of information.
In·for·ma·tion Ar·chi·tec·ture

# Graphis Books

| Books | USA/Canada* | Germany** | UK** | All other countries** |
|---|---|---|---|---|
| o The Human Condition: Photojournalism 97 | US$ 49.95 | DM 78,– | £ 42.00 | SFR. 69.– |
| o Information Architects | US$ 49.95 | DM 149,– | £ 52.00 | SFR. 123.– |
| o Graphis Advertising 97 | US$ 69.95 | DM 149,– | £ 52.00 | SFR. 123.– |
| o Graphis Annual Reports 5 | US$ 69.95 | DM 162,– | £ 55.00 | SFR. 137.– |
| o Graphis Book Design | US$ 75.95 | DM 162,– | £ 55.00 | SFR. 137.– |
| o Graphis Corporate Identity 2 | US$ 75.95 | DM 162,– | £ 55.00 | SFR. 137.– |
| o Graphis Design 98 | US$ 69.95 | DM 149,– | £ 52.00 | SFR. 123.– |
| o Graphis Digital Fonts | US$ 69.95 | DM 149,– | £ 52.00 | SFR. 123.– |
| o Graphis Ephemera | US$ 75.95 | DM 162,– | £ 55.00 | SFR. 137.– |
| o Graphis Fine Art Photography 2 | US$ 85.95 | DM 155,– | £ 69.00 | SFR. 128.– |
| o Graphis Letterhead 3 | US$ 75.00 | DM 162,– | £ 55.00 | SFR. 137.– |
| o Graphis Logo 3 | US$ 49.95 | DM 149,– | £ 52.00 | SFR. 123.– |
| o Graphis Music CDs | US$ 75.95 | DM 162,– | £ 55.00 | SFR. 137.– |
| o Graphis New Media 1 | US$ 75.00 | DM 162,– | £ 55.00 | SFR. 137.– |
| o Graphis Nudes 2 | US$ 50.00 | DM 71,– | £ 32.00 | SFR. 72.– |
| o Graphis Photo 97 | US$ 69.95 | DM 149,– | £ 52.00 | SFR. 123.– |
| o Graphis Poster 97 | US$ 69.95 | DM 149,– | £ 52.00 | SFR. 123.– |
| o Graphis Product Design 2 | US$ 69.95 | DM 149,– | £ 52.00 | SFR. 123.– |
| o Graphis Student Design 97 | US$ 49.95 | DM 71,– | £ 32.00 | SFR. 59.– |
| o Graphis Typography 2 | US$ 69.95 | DM 162,– | £ 55.00 | SFR. 137.– |
| o Graphis Type Specimens | US$ 49.95 | DM 89,– | £ 37.00 | SFR. 75.– |
| o World Trademarks 100 yrs. (2 vol. set) | US$ 250.00 | DM 458,– | £ 198.00 | SFR. 385.– |
| o Graphis Paper Specifier System (GPS) | US$ 495.00 | | | |

Shipping/Handling: Add $4 per book in USA and $10 per book outside USA

For GPS Shipping/Handling: Add $30 in USA and $100 outside USA

Note: NY residents add 8.25% sales tax

For orders from EC countries VAT will be charged

o Check enclosed (payable to Graphis)

o Charge my credit card:

o American Express

o MasterCard/Eurocard/Access

o Visa/BarclayCard/Carte Bleue

Card number      Expiration date

Cardholder name

Signature

(Please print)

Name

Title

Company

Address

City

State/province      Zip code.

Country      Phone

* Send order form and make check payable to: Graphis Inc., 141 Lexington Avenue, New York, NY 10016–8193, USA

**Please send order form to: Graphis Press Corp., Dufourstrasse 107, CH–8008 Zürich, Switzerland

Graphis 303

Graphis 303

Makela Lewis Moberly Sagmeister Newland Fallon McElligott Berlin Haase & Knebl

Graphis 304

Graphis 304

Schwab Illustrators Demachelier Koolhaas Kusabaya Stolichnaya Trickel

Graphis 305

Graphis 305

Johnson Conran IKEA Mead Show Grundy & Northedge Slover Tachibana

# Graphis Magazine

| Magazine | USA* | Canada* | South America/<br>Asia/Pacific** | Germany** | UK** | All other<br>countries** |
|---|---|---|---|---|---|---|
| ○ One year (6 issues) | US$ 89.00 | US$ 99.00 | US$ 125.00 | DM 190,– | £ 68.00 | SFR. 164.– |
| ○ Two years (12 issues) | US$ 159.00 | US$ 179.00 | US$ 235.00 | DM 342,– | £ 122.00 | SFR. 295.– |
| ○ Airmail surcharge (6 issues) | US$ 59.00 | US$ 59.00 | US$ 59.00 | DM 75,– | £ 30.00 | SFR. 65.– |
| ○ Registered mail | | | | DM 24,– | £ 9.00 | SFR. 20.– |

○ 33% discount for students with copy of valid, dated student ID and payment with order

○ Check enclosed (payable to Graphis)

○ Charge my credit card:

○ American Express

○ MasterCard/Eurocard/Access

○ Visa/BarclayCard/Carte Bleue

Card number _____ Expiration date _____

Cardholder name _____

Signature _____

○ Please bill me                    (Please print)

Name _____

Title _____

Company _____

Address _____

City _____

State/province _____ Zip code _____

Country _____ Phone _____

* Send order form and make check payable to: Graphis Inc., 141 Lexington Avenue, New York, NY 10016–8193, USA

**Please send order form to: Graphis Press Corp., Dufourstrasse 107, CH–8008 Zürich, Switzerland

Service begins with issue that is current when order is processed

exit